Experiencing theAmerican Civil War

Novels, Nonfiction Books, Short Stories, Poems, Plays, Films & Songs

EXPERIENCING
ERAS &
EVENTS

Experiencing the American Civil War

Novels, Nonfiction Books, Short Stories, Poems, Plays, Films & Songs

Kevin Hillstrom and
Laurie Collier Hillstrom
Lawrence W. Baker, Editor

Volume 1:
Novels
Nonfiction Books

GALE GROUP

THOMSON LEARNING

Detroit • New York • San Diego • San Francisco
Boston • New Haven, Conn. • Waterville, Maine
London • Munich

Experiencing the American Civil War

Kevin Hillstrom and Laurie Collier Hillstrom

Staff

Lawrence W. Baker, *U•X•L Senior Editor*
Carol DeKane Nagel, *U•X•L Managing Editor*
Tom Romig, *U•X•L Publisher*

Rita Wimberley, *Senior Buyer*
Evi Seoud, *Assistant Manager, Composition Purchasing and Electronic Prepress*

Pamela A. E. Galbreath, *Senior Art Director*

Edna Hedblad, *Permissions Specialist*
Kim Davis, *Permissions Associate*

Kelly A. Quin, *Editor, Imaging and Multimedia Content*
Pamela Reed, *Imaging Coordinator*
Leitha Etheridge-Sims, *Image Cataloger*
Robert Duncan, Dan Newell, Luke Rademacher, *Imaging Specialists*

Linda Mahoney, LM Design, *Typesetting*

Cover artwork: Harriette Gillem Robinet: Photograph by McLouis Robinet; reproduced by permission of Harriette Gillem Robinet. Walt Whitman: Photograph by Mathew Brady; courtesy of the National Archives and Records Administration. *Glory* scene: Reproduced by permission of the Kobal Collection. Battle of Chancellorsville scene: Lithograph by Currier and Ives; reproduced by permission of the Corbis Corporation.

Library of Congress Control Card Number: 2001096327

Copyright © 2002
U•X•L, an imprint of The Gale Group
27500 Drake Road
Farmington Hills, MI 48331-3535

TM This book is printed on acid-free paper that meets the minimum requirements of American National Standard for Information Sciences—Permanent Paper for Printed Library Materials, ANSI Z39.48-1984.

ISBN 0-7876-5585-6 (2-volume set)
ISBN 0-7876-5413-2 (volume 1)
ISBN 0-7876-5586-4 (volume 2)

Printed in the United States of America

10 9 8 7 6 5 4 3 2 1

Contents

Advisory Board

Special thanks are due to U•X•L's *Experiencing the American Civil War* advisors for their invaluable comments and suggestions:

Elaine Ezell, Library Media Specialist, Bowling Green Junior High School, Bowling Green, Ohio

Ann West LaPrise, Junior High/Elementary Media Specialist, Huron School District, New Boston, Michigan

Angela Leeper, Educational Consultant, Instructional Resources Evaluation Services, North Carolina Department of Public Instruction, Raleigh, North Carolina

Bonnie L. Raasch, Media Specialist, C. B. Vernon Middle School, Marion, Iowa

Reader's Guide

Experiencing the American Civil War: Novels, Nonfiction Books, Short Stories, Poems, Plays, Films, and Songs is a two-volume reference set that provides detailed information on twenty-five creative works about the Civil War era that young adult audiences would find interesting. Some of the works discussed in this collection were written, composed, or performed while the outcome of that great war was still in doubt. Others were created in the immediate aftermath of that conflict, when Northerner and Southerner alike looked over finally silent battlefields with mingled anger and sorrow. And still other works featured in this set were produced more than a century after the war ended. The creation and inclusion of these latter works reflects not only the Civil War's status as one of the pivotal events in American history, but also the conflict's enduring hold on the nation's imagination.

Experiencing the American Civil War is a resource that will help students understand the Civil War era. It will also guide them as they explore various films, novels, poems, and other creative works that highlight specific events, issues, personalities, and themes associated with that turbulent period of

American history. Indeed, many of the works covered in this set are already commonly utilized as teaching tools in today's classrooms, while others address subjects—slavery, Reconstruction, the wartime experiences of ordinary "Rebels" and "Yankees," Gettysburg and other major battles—that are frequently highlighted in U.S. history curricula.

Many of the essays are also supplemented with informative sidebars that provide additional insights into the creative work or Civil War event under discussion. Other features of *Experiencing the American Civil War* include a timeline that lists important events of the Civil War era; a bibliography of general Civil War sources, including notable Internet sites; and a comprehensive subject index.

Organization of *Experiencing the American Civil War*

The twenty-five essays included in *Experiencing the American Civil War* are arranged by genre. Each of the seven genre sections contained in the set—novels, nonfiction books, short stories, poems, plays, films, and songs—begins with an overview of Civil War–related works of that genre, including brief annotations of specific works that are noteworthy in one respect or another. Some of these works are intended for general audiences, but many are specifically tailored for children or young adult readers. Following each overview essay, two to seven essays provide detailed analysis of specific works in that genre. Each work discussed includes the following sections:

- Identification and summary of the work

- Biographical information on the author, composer, or director of the work

- Historical background on the issues, events, and/or personalties highlighted in the work, including comments on the work's relationship to historical facts

- Plot and character summary or, for poems, an analysis of subject matter

- Major themes and stylistic characteristics of the work

- Research and activity ideas that explore different facets of the work

- List of related titles in various genres

- Guide to sources—books, magazine articles, and Internet sites—containing additional information on the work and the specific Civil War issues it addresses

Inclusion Criteria

Several criteria were considered in the selection of works to be featured in *Experiencing the American Civil War*. We included several of the nation's most enduring works about the Civil War—such as the novel *The Red Badge of Courage* and the film *Gone with the Wind*—which are suitable for students. We also strove to include works featuring young characters with whom students can identify. Balance was another important factor in the final makeup of the book. Northern and Southern perspectives are both well-represented, and care was also taken to include works from white and black outlooks and male and female viewpoints. Finally, *Experiencing the American Civil War* was compiled with an eye toward providing users with information on diverse issues and events associated with the Civil War. For example, subjects explored in this collection range from the lonely, perilous life of Civil War scouts (detailed in Jack London's short story "War") to the legendary performance of the Union's all-black Fifty-fourth Massachusetts Regiment (showcased in the film *Glory*) to the assassination of President Abraham Lincoln (recalled in Walt Whitman's poem "O Captain! My Captain!").

Acknowledgments

The authors and editor wish to thank copyeditor Theresa Murray, proofreader Amy Marcaccio Keyzer, and typesetter Linda Mahoney of LM Design for their fine work.

Comments and Suggestions

We welcome your comments on *Experiencing the American Civil War*. Please send correspondence to: Editors, *Experiencing the American Civil War*, U•X•L, 27500 Drake Rd., Farmington Hills, MI 48331-3535; call toll-free: 800-877-4253; fax to 248-414-5043; or send e-mail via www.galegroup.com.

American Civil War Timeline

1775 Philadelphia Quakers organize America's first antislavery society.

1776–83 English colonies' War for Independence against Great Britain ends with the formation of the United States.

1788 The U.S. Constitution is ratified, providing legal protection to slaveowners.

1814 Wilmer McLean, the Virginia merchant who saw both the beginning and end of the Civil War take place on his property, is born.

1815 Daniel Decatur Emmett, the musician who composed the song "Dixie," is born in Mount Vernon, Ohio.

1818 Frederick Douglass is born a slave in Maryland.

1789
George
Washington takes
office as the first
U.S. president.

1775
"Yankee Doodle"
is written.

1818
Congress
adopts a
U.S. flag.

| 1760 | 1780 | 1800 | 1820 |

1819 Julia Ward Howe, the poet who wrote the words to the song "Battle Hymn of the Republic," is born in New York City.

1819 Poet Walt Whitman, who wrote "O Captain! My Captain!," is born on Long Island, New York.

1820 Congress passes the Missouri Compromise, which maintains the balance between slave and free states in the Union.

1820 Harriet Tubman is born a slave in Maryland.

1823 Civil War photographer Mathew Brady is born in Warren County, New York.

1823 Civil War diarist Mary Chesnut is born in Statesburg, South Carolina.

1826 Canada officially refuses to return escaped slaves to the United States, making America's northern neighbor a prime destination for runaways on the Underground Railroad.

1833 The Female Anti-Slavery Society and the American Anti-Slavery Society are founded.

1835 Samuel Langhorne Clemens (Mark Twain), author of the short story "The Private History of a Campaign That Failed," is born in Florida, Missouri.

1836 Bret Harte, author of the poem "John Burns of Gettysburg," is born in Albany, New York.

1837 Robert Gould Shaw, who becomes commander of the all-black Fifty-fourth Massachusetts Regiment in the Union Army, is born in Boston, Massachusetts.

1838 Frederick Douglass escapes from slavery and becomes a famous speaker and abolitionist.

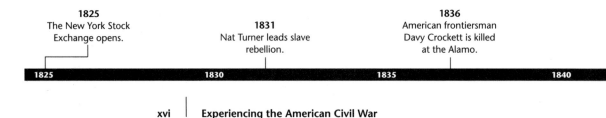

1825
The New York Stock Exchange opens.

1831
Nat Turner leads slave rebellion.

1836
American frontiersman Davy Crockett is killed at the Alamo.

| 1825 | 1830 | 1835 | 1840 |

1842   Civil War soldier and poet Sidney Lanier is born in Macon, Georgia.

1842   Writer Ambrose Bierce is born in Meigs County, Ohio.

1849   Harriet Tubman escapes from slavery and becomes a famous "conductor" on the Underground Railroad.

1850   The Fugitive Slave Act increases antislavery feelings in the North.

1852   Harriet Beecher Stowe's novel *Uncle Tom's Cabin* is published, increasing support for the abolitionist movement in the North.

1854   The Kansas-Nebraska Act is passed, returning decisions about allowing slavery back to individual states.

1857   The U.S. Supreme Court issues its famous *Dred Scott* decision, which increases Northern fears about the spread of slavery.

1859   Abolitionist John Brown leads a raid on Harper's Ferry, Virginia, in an unsuccessful effort to start a slave revolt across the South.

1859   Daniel Decatur Emmett composes the song "Dixie."

May 18, 1860   The Republican Party nominates Abraham Lincoln as its candidate for president.

November 6, 1860   Abraham Lincoln is elected president of the United States in the 1860 elections.

December 20, 1860   South Carolina secedes from the Union.

January 9, 1861   Mississippi secedes from the Union.

January 10, 1861   Florida secedes from the Union.

January 11, 1861   Alabama secedes from the Union.

1844
Samuel F. B. Morse transmits the first telegraph message.

1851
The New York Times begins publication.

1859
Charles Darwin publishes his theory of evolution.

1845   1850   1855   1860

American Civil War Timeline | xvii

January 19, 1861 Georgia secedes from the Union.

January 26, 1861 Louisiana secedes from the Union.

January 29, 1861 Kansas is admitted into the Union as the thirty-fourth state.

February 1, 1861 Texas secedes from the Union.

February 8, 1861 The Confederate Constitution is adopted in Montgomery, Alabama.

February 18, 1861 Jefferson Davis is inaugurated as the president of the Confederacy.

March 4, 1861 Abraham Lincoln is inaugurated as the sixteenth president of the United States.

April 12, 1861 South Carolina troops open fire on Fort Sumter, marking the beginning of the American Civil War.

April 13, 1861 Union major Robert Anderson surrenders Fort Sumter to the Confederates.

May 6, 1861 Arkansas secedes from the Union.

May 7, 1861 Tennessee forms an alliance with the Confederacy that makes it a Confederate state for all practical purposes.

May 20, 1861 North Carolina secedes from the Union.

May 23, 1861 Virginia secedes from the Union.

June 3, 1861 U.S. senator Stephen A. Douglas of Illinois dies in Chicago.

June 11, 1861 Counties in western Virginia resist Virginia's vote to secede and set up their own government, which is loyal to the Union.

July 20, 1861 The Confederate Congress convenes at the Confederate capital of Richmond, Virginia.

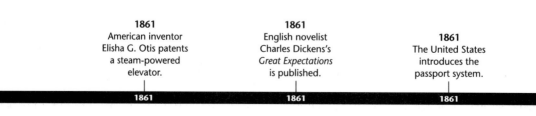

1861
American inventor
Elisha G. Otis patents
a steam-powered
elevator.

1861
English novelist
Charles Dickens's
Great Expectations
is published.

1861
The United States
introduces the
passport system.

1861   1861   1861

July 21, 1861 Confederate forces win the First Battle of Bull Run (also known as the First Battle of Manassas), the war's first major battle.

1862 Julia Ward Howe's song "Battle Hymn of the Republic" appears in *Atlantic Monthly* magazine.

February 6, 1862 Union general Ulysses S. Grant captures Fort Henry on the Tennessee River.

February 16, 1862 Union general Ulysses S. Grant captures Fort Donelson on the Cumberland River.

February 25, 1862 Confederates abandon Nashville, Tennessee, to oncoming Union forces.

April 6–7, 1862 Union and Confederate forces battle in the inconclusive Battle of Shiloh in Tennessee.

April 16, 1862 The Confederate Congress passes a conscription act requiring most able-bodied men between the ages of eighteen and thirty-five to sign up for military service.

April 25, 1862 Union fleet under the command of Admiral David Farragut captures New Orleans, Louisiana.

June 1, 1862 General Robert E. Lee assumes command of Confederate forces defending Richmond, Virginia.

June 6, 1862 Union forces take control of Memphis, Tennessee.

June 17, 1862 Confederate forces led by Thomas "Stonewall" Jackson leave the Shenandoah Valley after a successful military campaign.

June 25, 1862 The Seven Days' Battles begin between Union general George McClellan's Army of the Potomac and Confederate general Robert E. Lee's Army of Northern Virginia.

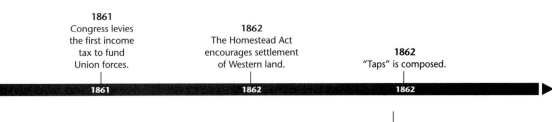

1861
Congress levies the first income tax to fund Union forces.

1862
The Homestead Act encourages settlement of Western land.

1862
"Taps" is composed.

1861   1862   1862

August 29–30, 1862 The Second Battle of Bull Run ends in a disastrous defeat for the Union.

September 5, 1862 Confederate general Robert E. Lee leads the Army of Northern Virginia into Northern territory for the first time, as his force enters Maryland.

September 15, 1862 Stonewall Jackson's army captures twelve thousand Union troops at Harper's Ferry, Virginia.

September 17, 1862 Union general George McClellan's Army of the Potomac and Confederate general Robert E. Lee's Army of Northern Virginia fight at Antietam in the bloodiest single day of the war. Neither side registers a conclusive victory, but the draw convinces Lee to return to Virginia.

September 22, 1862 President Abraham Lincoln issues his preliminary Emancipation Proclamation, which will free slaves in Confederate territory.

November 7, 1862 President Abraham Lincoln removes General George McClellan from command of the Army of the Potomac, replacing him with General Ambrose Burnside.

December 13, 1862 General Robert E. Lee's Confederate forces hand the Union a decisive defeat at the Battle of Fredericksburg.

January 1, 1863 President Abraham Lincoln issues the Emancipation Proclamation, which frees all slaves in Confederate territory.

January 2, 1863 Union victory at the Battle of Stones River stops Confederate plans to invade middle Tennessee.

January 23, 1863 General Ambrose Burnside's new offensive against Robert E. Lee's Army of Northern Virginia sput-

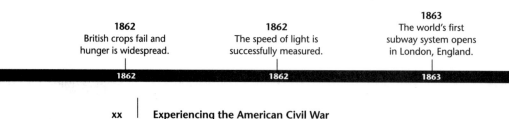

1862
British crops fail and
hunger is widespread.

1862
The speed of light is
successfully measured.

1863
The world's first
subway system opens
in London, England.

1862

1862

1863

ters to a halt in bad weather. Burnside's "Mud March" convinces President Abraham Lincoln to replace him with General Joseph Hooker.

February 1863 The all-black Fifty-fourth Massachusetts Regiment is organized under the leadership of Colonel Robert Gould Shaw.

March 3, 1863 U.S. Congress passes a conscription act requiring most able-bodied Northern men to sign up for military service.

April 2, 1863 Bread riots erupt in Richmond, Virginia, as hungry civilians resort to violence to feed their families.

May 2, 1863 General Robert E. Lee and the Confederates claim a big victory in the Battle of Chancellorsville, but Stonewall Jackson is killed during the battle.

May 22, 1863 General Ulysses S. Grant begins the siege of Vicksburg, Mississippi, after attempts to take the Confederate stronghold by force are turned back.

June 20, 1863 West Virginia is admitted into the Union as the thirty-fifth state.

July 1–3, 1863 The famous Battle of Gettysburg takes place in Pennsylvania. Union general George Meade and the Army of the Potomac successfully turn back General Robert E. Lee's attempted invasion of the North, doing terrible damage to Lee's Army of Northern Virginia in the process.

July 4, 1863 Vicksburg surrenders to General Ulysses S. Grant and his Union force after a six-week siege of the city.

July 9, 1863 Union troops take control of Port Hudson, Louisiana. The victory gives the North control of the Mississippi River.

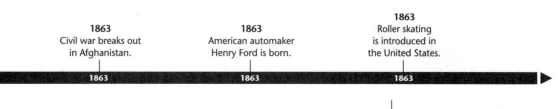

1863	1863	1863
Civil war breaks out in Afghanistan.	American automaker Henry Ford is born.	Roller skating is introduced in the United States.

| 1863 | 1863 | 1863 |

July 13, 1863 Anti-draft mobs begin four days of rioting in New York City.

July 18, 1863 The all-black Fifty-fourth Massachusetts Regiment leads the attack on Fort Wagner in South Carolina.

August 21, 1863 Confederate raiders led by William C. Quantrill murder 150 antislavery settlers and burn large sections of Lawrence, Kansas.

September 2, 1863 Union troops take control of Knoxville, Tennessee.

September 9, 1863 Union forces take control of Chattanooga, Tennessee, after the city is abandoned by General Braxton Bragg's army.

September 20, 1863 The two-day Battle of Chickamauga in Georgia ends in a major defeat for the Union.

September 23, 1863 General Braxton Bragg begins the Confederate siege of Chattanooga, Tennessee.

October 17, 1863 General Ulysses S. Grant is named supreme commander of Union forces in the west.

November 19, 1863 President Abraham Lincoln delivers his famous Gettysburg Address at a ceremony dedicating a cemetery for soldiers who died at the Battle of Gettysburg.

November 25, 1863 The three-day Battle of Chattanooga results in a major victory for the North, as Union troops led by General George Thomas scatter General Braxton Bragg's Confederate army.

December 8, 1863 President Abraham Lincoln proposes his Ten Percent Plan, which says that seceded states can return to the Union provided that one-tenth of the

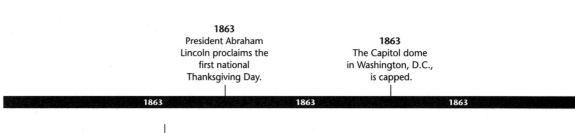

1863
President Abraham Lincoln proclaims the first national Thanksgiving Day.

1863
The Capitol dome in Washington, D.C., is capped.

1863   1863   1863

1860 voters agree to form a state government that is loyal to the Union.

December 27, 1863 General Joseph Johnston takes command of the Confederate Army of Tennessee.

March 12, 1864 General Ulysses S. Grant is promoted to leadership of all of the Union armies.

March 18, 1864 General William T. Sherman is named to lead Union armies in the west.

April 12, 1864 Confederate troops led by Nathan Bedford Forrest capture Fort Pillow, Tennessee, and are accused of murdering black Union soldiers stationed there.

April 17, 1864 Union general Ulysses S. Grant calls a halt to prisoner exchanges between North and South, further increasing the Confederacy's manpower problems.

May 5, 1864 General Robert E. Lee's Army of Northern Virginia and General Ulysses S. Grant's Army of the Potomac battle in the Wilderness campaign.

May 9–12, 1864 General Robert E. Lee stops the Union advance on Richmond at the brutal Battle of Spotsylvania.

June 3, 1864 The Union's Army of the Potomac suffers heavy losses in a failed assault on Robert E. Lee's army at Cold Harbor, Virginia.

June 18, 1864 General Ulysses S. Grant begins the Union siege of Petersburg, which is defended by Robert E. Lee's Army of Northern Virginia.

June 23, 1864 Confederate forces led by Jubal Early begin a campaign in the Shenandoah Valley.

July 11, 1864 Confederate troops commanded by Jubal Early reach the outskirts of Washington, D.C., before being forced to return to the Shenandoah Valley.

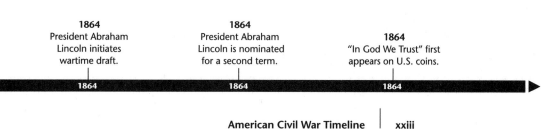

1864
President Abraham Lincoln initiates wartime draft.

1864

1864
President Abraham Lincoln is nominated for a second term.

1864

1864
"In God We Trust" first appears on U.S. coins.

1864

July 17, 1864 General John Bell Hood takes command of the Confederate Army of Tennessee.

August 1864 Congress grants black soldiers in the Union army pay equal to that of white soldiers.

August 5, 1864 Admiral David Farragut leads the Union navy to a major victory in the Battle of Mobile Bay, which closes off one of the Confederacy's last remaining ports.

August 29, 1864 The Democratic Party nominates General George McClellan as its candidate for president of the United States and pushes a campaign promising an end to the war.

September 1, 1864 General William T. Sherman captures Atlanta, Georgia, after a long campaign.

September 4, 1864 General William T. Sherman orders all civilians to leave Atlanta, Georgia, as a way to hurt Southern morale.

September 19–22, 1864 Union troops led by Philip Sheridan defeat Jubal Early's Confederate army in the Shenandoah Valley.

October 6, 1864 Philip Sheridan's Union troops begin a campaign of destruction in the Shenandoah Valley in order to wipe out Confederate sympathizers and sources of supplies.

October 19, 1864 Philip Sheridan's army drives Jubal Early's Confederate force out of the Shenandoah Valley following the Battle of Cedar Creek.

October 31, 1864 Nevada is admitted into the Union as the thirty-sixth state.

November 8, 1864 Abraham Lincoln is reelected to the presidency of the United States by a comfortable margin.

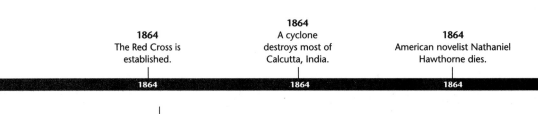

1864
The Red Cross is established.

1864
A cyclone destroys most of Calcutta, India.

1864
American novelist Nathaniel Hawthorne dies.

1864   1864   1864

November 15, 1864 General William T. Sherman begins his famous March to the Sea, in which his Union army destroys a large area of Georgia on its way to the port city of Savannah.

December 16, 1864 Union forces under the command of General George Thomas crush John Bell Hood's Army of Tennessee at the Battle of Nashville.

December 21, 1864 William T. Sherman's Union army completes its March to the Sea by taking control of Savannah, Georgia.

January 1865 General William T. Sherman issues Field Order 15, which grants land to former slaves in the South.

January 31, 1865 The U.S. Congress submits the Thirteenth Amendment, which abolishes slavery, to the individual states for passage.

February 17, 1865 General William T. Sherman's army occupies the South Carolina capital of Columbia.

February 18, 1865 Union forces seize control of Charleston, South Carolina.

February 22, 1865 Confederate president Jefferson Davis returns command of the Army of Tennessee to General Joseph Johnston in a desperate attempt to stop William T. Sherman's advance into North Carolina.

March 2, 1865 Remaining Confederate troops in the Shenandoah Valley go down to defeat at the hands of Philip Sheridan.

March 4, 1865 President Abraham Lincoln is inaugurated for a second term of office.

March 13, 1865 The Confederate Congress authorizes the use of slaves as Confederate combat soldiers.

1864
Pasteurization is invented.

1864

1865
Lewis Carroll writes
*Alice's Adventures
in Wonderland.*

1865

1865
Civil War balloonist
Thaddeus Lowe invents
the ice machine.

1865

April 1–2, 1865 Ulysses S. Grant's Army of the Potomac successfully breaks through Confederate defenses at Petersburg, forcing Robert E. Lee's Army of Northern Virginia to evacuate the city and give up its defense of Richmond.

April 3, 1865 Union troops take control of Richmond, Virginia.

April 9, 1865 Trapped by pursuing Federal troops, General Robert E. Lee surrenders to General Ulysses S. Grant at Appomattox Court House, Virginia.

April 14, 1865 President Abraham Lincoln is shot by John Wilkes Booth while attending a play at Ford's Theatre in Washington, D.C.

April 15, 1865 Vice president Andrew Johnson becomes president after Abraham Lincoln dies.

April 18, 1865 Confederate general Joseph Johnston surrenders his Army of Tennessee to William T. Sherman near Raleigh, North Carolina.

April 26, 1865 John Wilkes Booth is killed by Federal soldiers in a barn near Bowling Green, Virginia.

May 1865 The Freedmen's Bureau begins giving forty acres of land to former slave families in the South; forty thousand people take advantage of the program to start their own farms.

May 10, 1865 Confederate president Jefferson Davis is taken prisoner by Federal troops at Irwinsville, Georgia.

May 10, 1865 President Andrew Johnson announces the end of armed resistance in the South.

September 1865 The Freedman's Bureau begins taking away land formerly granted to slave families.

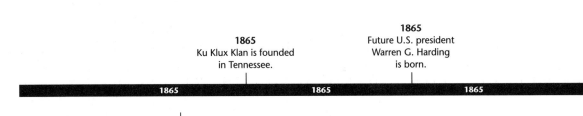

1865
Ku Klux Klan is founded
in Tennessee.

1865
Future U.S. president
Warren G. Harding
is born.

1865   1865   1865

October 1865 Walt Whitman publishes *Drum Taps,* a book of Civil War poetry that includes "O Captain! My Captain!," a tribute to assassinated president Abraham Lincoln.

1866 The Republican Congress passes a Civil Rights Act over President Andrew Johnson's veto. The Act gives citizenship and other rights to black people.

1866 Race riots between blacks and whites erupt during the summer in Memphis, Tennessee, and New Orleans, Louisiana.

1866 Tennessee is readmitted into the Union by Congress.

1867 Congress passes the Military Reconstruction Act over President Andrew Johnson's veto.

1867 The Ku Klux Klan adopts a formal constitution and selects former Confederate general Nathan Bedford Forrest as its first leader.

1867 Former Confederate president Jefferson Davis is released from a Virginia jail after two years of imprisonment.

1868 Political disagreements between Congress and President Andrew Johnson become so great that the president is impeached. He escapes being removed from office by one vote in his Senate impeachment trial.

1868 Congress passes the Fifteenth Amendment, which extends voting rights to blacks, and sends the bill along to individual states for ratification.

1868 Alabama, Arkansas, Florida, Louisiana, North Carolina, and South Carolina are readmitted into the Union by Congress.

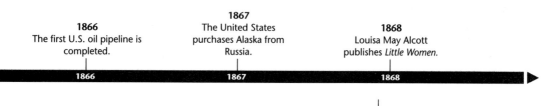

1866
The first U.S. oil pipeline is completed.

1867
The United States purchases Alaska from Russia.

1868
Louisa May Alcott publishes *Little Women.*

1866   1867   1868

1868 Republican Ulysses S. Grant is elected the eighteenth president of the United States.

1870 The Fifteenth Amendment, guaranteeing voting rights for blacks, is ratified by the states and becomes law.

1870 Congress passes the Enforcement Act of 1870 in an effort to protect the voting rights of all citizens—especially blacks—in the South.

1870 Georgia, Mississippi, Texas, and Virginia are readmitted into the Union by Congress.

1871 Congress passes the Ku Klux Klan Act, which outlaws conspiracies, use of disguises, and other practices of the white supremacist group.

1871 Stephen Crane, author of the novel *The Red Badge of Courage,* is born in Newark, New Jersey.

1872 Ulysses S. Grant is reelected president of the United States.

1872 John Burns, known as the "hero of Gettysburg," dies.

1875 Congress passes a Civil Rights Act barring discrimination in hotels, theaters, railroads, and other public places.

1876 Republican Rutherford B. Hayes and Democrat Samuel J. Tilden run a very close race for the presidency of the United States. Tilden wins the popular vote, but neither candidate receives enough electoral votes for election. The two political parties eventually agree to a compromise in which Hayes becomes president in exchange for a guarantee that he remove federal troops from Florida, Louisiana, and South Carolina.

1876 Jack London, author of the short story "War," is born in San Francisco, California.

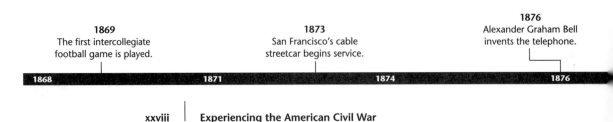

1869
The first intercollegiate football game is played.

1873
San Francisco's cable streetcar begins service.

1876
Alexander Graham Bell invents the telephone.

1868   1871   1874   1876

1877 President Rutherford B. Hayes removes Federal troops from the South. This withdrawal increases the vulnerability of blacks to Southern racism and marks the end of the Reconstruction period in American history.

1881 Civil War soldier and poet Sidney Lanier dies.

1882 Wilmer McLean, the subject of Ann Rinaldi's novel *In My Father's House,* dies.

1885 Mark Twain's short story "The Private History of a Campaign That Failed" is published in *Century Magazine.*

1886 Civil War diarist Mary Chesnut dies.

1891 Ambrose Bierce's short story "An Occurrence at Owl Creek Bridge" is published in his collection *Tales of Soldiers and Civilians.*

1892 Poet Walt Whitman dies.

1895 Abolitionist Frederick Douglass dies.

1895 Stephen Crane's novel *The Red Badge of Courage* is published.

1896 Civil War photographer Mathew Brady dies.

1900 Thomas Wolfe, author of the short story "Chickamauga," is born in Asheville, North Carolina.

1900 Author Stephen Crane dies.

1902 Poet Bret Harte dies.

1902 David O. Selznick, producer of the film *Gone with the Wind,* is born in Pittsburgh, Pennsylvania.

1904 "Dixie" composer Daniel Decatur Emmett dies.

1907 Irene Hunt, author of *Across Five Aprils,* is born in Pontiac, Illinois.

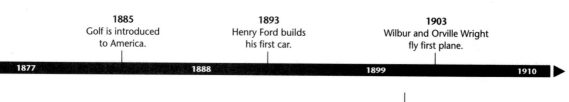

1885
Golf is introduced to America.

1893
Henry Ford builds his first car.

1903
Wilbur and Orville Wright fly first plane.

1877   1888   1899   1910

1910	Poet Julia Ward Howe dies.
1910	Writer Samuel Langhorne Clemens (Mark Twain) dies.
1910	Jack London's short story "War" is published in *The Nation.*
1912	Patricia Clapp, author of the novel *The Tamarack Tree,* is born in Boston, Massachusetts.
1913	Underground Railroad "conductor" Harriet Tubman dies.
1913	Writer Ambrose Bierce disappears in Mexico.
1916	Writer Jack London dies.
1917	Ossie Davis, author of the play *Escape to Freedom,* is born in Cogdell, Georgia.
1928	James Lincoln Collier, co-author of *With Every Drop of Blood,* is born in New York City.
1930	Christopher Collier, co-author of *With Every Drop of Blood,* is born in New York City.
1931	Harriette Gillem Robinet, author of *Forty Acres and Maybe a Mule,* is born in Washington, D.C.
1934	Ann Rinaldi, author of *In My Father's House,* is born in New York City.
1938	Writer Thomas Wolfe dies.
1939	The film *Gone with the Wind* is released.
1939	Gary Paulsen, author of the novel *Soldier's Heart,* is born in Minneapolis, Minnesota.
1941	Thomas Wolfe's story "Chickamauga" is published in his collection *The Hills Beyond.*

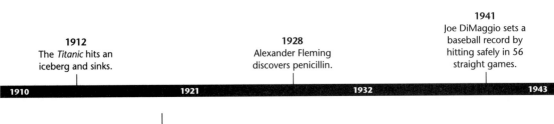

1912
The *Titanic* hits an iceberg and sinks.

1928
Alexander Fleming discovers penicillin.

1941
Joe DiMaggio sets a baseball record by hitting safely in 56 straight games.

1910   1921   1932   1943

1944	Robbie Robertson, the songwriter who composed "The Night They Drove Old Dixie Down," is born in Toronto, Ontario, Canada.
1946	Gena K. Gorrell, author of *North Star to Freedom,* is born in Toronto, Ontario, Canada.
1947	Jim Murphy, author of *The Boys' War,* is born in Newark, New Jersey.
1947	Zak Mettger, author of *Till Victory Is Won,* is born in Washington, D.C.
1951	Andrew Hudgins, the poet who wrote "After the Wilderness," is born in Killeen, Texas.
1952	William B. Becker, author of the play *Brady of Broadway,* is born.
1952	Edward Zwick, director of the film *Glory,* is born in Chicago, Illinois.
1964	Irene Hunt's novel *Across Five Aprils* is published.
1965	Film director David O. Selznick dies.
1969	The song "The Night They Drove Old Dixie Down" is recorded by the Band.
1976	Ossie Davis's play *Escape to Freedom* is published.
1981	The nonfiction book *Mary Chesnut's Civil War* is published.
1986	Patricia Clapp's novel *The Tamarack Tree* is published.
1988	Andrew Hudgins's poem "After the Wilderness" is published in his collection *After the Lost War: A Narrative.*
1989	Edward Zwick's film *Glory* is released.
1990	Jim Murphy's nonfiction book *The Boys' War* is published.

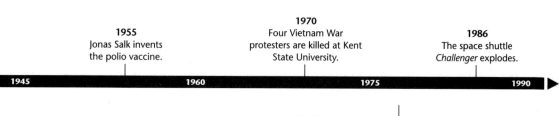

1955
Jonas Salk invents the polio vaccine.

1970
Four Vietnam War protesters are killed at Kent State University.

1986
The space shuttle *Challenger* explodes.

1945   1960   1975   1990

1991 William B. Becker's play *Brady of Broadway* is first produced.

1993 Ann Rinaldi's novel *In My Father's House* is published.

1994 James Lincoln Collier and Christopher Collier publish their novel *With Every Drop of Blood.*

1994 Zak Mettger's nonfiction book *Till Victory Is Won* is published.

1996 Gena Gorrell's nonfiction book *North Star to Freedom* is published.

1998 Harriette Gillem Robinet's novel *Forty Acres and Maybe a Mule* is published.

1998 Gary Paulsen's novel *Soldier's Heart* is published.

2001 Author Irene Hunt dies.

2001 Alice Randall's controversial novel *The Wind Done Gone,* based on *Gone with the Wind,* is published.

1993
Toni Morrison becomes the first African American to win the Nobel Prize in literature.

1997
U.S. president Bill Clinton is elected to a second term.

2000
Lavish worldwide celebrations usher in the new year.

1990 1994 1997 2001

American Civil War Novels

The American Civil War (1861–65) has probably inspired more writers than any other event in American history. The great national crisis captured people's imagination and seemed to stimulate them to create works of literature. During the war years, fictional works about the conflict appeared in newspapers and magazines and were published as books or pamphlets. These works ranged from sentimental novels about loss and longing, to sensational tales of battle, to children's stories about heroes and villains. Popular literature about the Civil War was often sold at stands on street corners and sometimes even in saloons.

Civil War fiction helped shape readers' feelings about the events of the war and the political issues behind it. In contrast to the literature of later wars, which tended to be more bitter, most novels and stories written during the Civil War had a patriotic tone. As the conflict dragged on, literature helped change people's attitudes about the capabilities of African Americans and women.

Many great American writers lived during the Civil War and composed poems, stories, essays, or novels about the conflict, including Ambrose Bierce, Nathaniel Hawthorne, Henry James, Herman Melville, and Mark Twain. One of the most important works of the Civil War era was *Uncle Tom's Cabin* by Harriet Beecher Stowe. This 1852 novel sold over two million copies in the years leading up to the Civil War. By presenting a vivid picture of the evils of slavery, it convinced countless Northerners to join the abolitionist movement and contributed to the divisions between North and South that led to the Civil War. Several other classic novels were published after the war ended. Examples include *The Red Badge of Courage* by Stephen Crane, an 1895 novel that follows the combat experiences of an individual soldier, and *Gone with the Wind* by Margaret Mitchell, a 1936 novel that follows the wartime struggles of a Southern belle.

The Civil War has also served as a topic for many modern writers, including some of America's best writers for young adults. Notable authors such as Patricia Beatty, Paul Fleischman, Irene Hunt, Kathryn Lasky, Patricia C. McKissack, Gary Paulsen, and Ann Rinaldi have all written novels set in the Civil War era.

Young adult novels about the Civil War cover a variety of topics. Some works center around the war's effect on civilians who live near battle sites and soldiers' families left at home. Examples include *Across Five Aprils* by Irene Hunt, *In My Father's House* by Ann Rinaldi, *The Tamarack Tree* by Patricia Clapp, and *Across the Lines* by Carolyn Reeder. Other novels talk about the wartime experiences of soldiers, scouts, spies, and other participants. Examples include *Soldier's Heart* by Gary Paulsen, *Bull Run* by Paul Fleischman, *The Journal of James Edmond Pease* by Jim Murphy, *Charley Skedaddle* by Patricia Beatty, *Red Cap* by G. Clifton Wisler, and *Girl in Blue* by Ann Rinaldi.

Many young adult novels set in the Civil War era tackle the topics of slavery, the Underground Railroad, and the service of black soldiers in the Union army. Examples include *With Every Drop of Blood* by James Lincoln Collier and Christopher Collier, *A Picture of Freedom* by Patricia C. McKissack, *Nightjohn* by Gary Paulsen, and *Who Comes with Cannons?* by Patricia Beatty. A few novels take place after the end of the war, as the North and the South struggled to become one nation again. Examples include *Forty Acres and Maybe a Mule* by Har-

riette Gillem Robinet, *Shades of Gray* by Carolyn Reeder, and *I Thought My Soul Would Rise and Fly* by Joyce Hansen.

Seven novels are featured in *Experiencing the American Civil War. Across Five Aprils,* by Irene Hunt, tells the story of the Civil War from the perspective of an Illinois farm boy, Jethro Creighton. Jethro stays at home and works on his family's farm while his brothers go off to fight in the war. He follows the conflict—which lasted from April 1861 to April 1865—through letters and newspaper articles.

In My Father's House, by Ann Rinaldi, follows the course of the Civil War from the perspective of a young Southern girl, Oscie Mason, who gets a close-up view of two important events in the conflict: the First Battle of Bull Run in 1861 and Confederate general Robert E. Lee's surrender at Appomattox in 1865. The first major battle of the war takes place on her Virginia plantation in 1861. Hoping to avoid further conflict, Oscie's family moves two hundred miles away to quiet Appomattox County. But in 1865, Oscie's new home becomes the site of the historic meeting at which Lee surrendered to Union general Ulysses S. Grant.

Patricia Clapp's novel *The Tamarack Tree* also shows the effect of the war on civilians. This book tells the story of Rosemary Leigh, an English teenager who experiences the siege of Vicksburg, Mississippi, in 1863. Rosemary, an outsider who has mixed feelings about the war, describes the terrible fear and hunger experienced by the residents of Vicksburg during the siege.

Another featured novel is *The Red Badge of Courage* by Stephen Crane. This famous work describes the experiences and emotions of one Union soldier who takes part in an unnamed but bloody battle of the Civil War. It was one of the first works of fiction to realistically explore emotions such as courage and fear on the battlefield.

Gary Paulsen's novel *Soldier's Heart* also follows the combat experiences of a young soldier. It is based on the actual Civil War experiences of Charley Goddard, a twelve-year-old boy who fought for the Union army as a member of the First Minnesota Volunteers. Paulsen shows the full horror of war by describing not only the blood and gore of combat but its emotional impact on young Charley.

With Every Drop of Blood, by James Lincoln Collier and Christopher Collier, takes place during the final weeks of the Civil War. It tells the story of Johnny, a fourteen-year-old farm boy from the Shenandoah Valley region of Virginia who is captured by a Union soldier named Cush Turner, a black boy about his own age. The novel shows how Johnny and Cush overcome their distrust and become friends.

Harriette Gillem Robinet's novel *Forty Acres and Maybe a Mule* takes place immediately after the end of the Civil War, during the period in American history known as Reconstruction. It tells the story of a fictional group of former slaves who briefly have the chance to farm their own land. Robinet shows the hope and disappointment of the Reconstruction era through the eyes of a twelve-year-old black boy named Pascal.

Representative Novels about the Civil War

Beatty, Patricia. *Charley Skedaddle.* New York: Morrow, 1987. *A novel about a twelve-year-old boy from New York City who joins the Union army as a drummer but then deserts his unit after realizing the horrors of combat.*

Beatty, Patricia. *Who Comes with Cannons?* New York: Morrow Junior Books, 1992. *A novel about a twelve-year-old Quaker girl living with relatives in North Carolina who run a station on the Underground Railroad.*

Clapp, Patricia. *The Tamarack Tree.* New York: Lothrop, Lee & Shepard, 1986. *Through the eyes of an outsider—an English teenager who experiences the siege of Vicksburg, Mississippi, in 1863—this book shows the effect of the war on civilians.*

Collier, James Lincoln, and Christopher Collier. *With Every Drop of Blood.* New York: Delacorte Press, 1994. *This novel tells the story of a fourteen-year-old farm boy who is captured by a Union soldier, a black boy about his own age.*

Crane, Stephen. *The Red Badge of Courage.* New York: D. Appleton, 1895. Multiple subsequent editions. *A novel that follows the combat experiences of an individual soldier.*

Fleischman, Paul. *Bull Run.* New York: HarperCollins Publishers, 1993. *A novel in which sixteen different characters tell about their experiences during the first major battle of the Civil War.*

Hansen, Joyce. *I Thought My Soul Would Rise and Fly.* New York: Scholastic, 1997. *This novel presents some similarities between a recently freed slave and an Irish immigrant settling in Massachusetts.*

Hansen, Joyce. *Which Way Freedom.* New York: Walker, 1986. *In this novel, an African American boy escapes from slavery and joins a black regiment of the Union army.*

Hunt, Irene. *Across Five Aprils*. Chicago: Follett, 1964. *A novel that tells the story of the Civil War from the perspective of an Illinois farm boy.*

McKissack, Patricia C. *A Picture of Freedom: The Diary of Clotee, a Slave Girl, Belmont Plantation*. New York: Scholastic, 1997. *A novel about an African American girl who tries to understand the true meaning of freedom.*

Mitchell, Margaret. *Gone with the Wind*. New York: Macmillan, 1936. Multiple subsequent editions. *An epic novel about the life of a wealthy young Southern woman during and after the Civil War.*

Murphy, Jim. *The Journal of James Edmond Pease, a Civil War Union Soldier*. New York: Scholastic, 1998. *In this novel, a sixteen-year-old Union soldier keeps a journal about the hardships of war and his experiences in battle.*

Paulsen, Gary. *Nightjohn*. New York: Delacorte Press, 1993. *A novel about a former slave who gives up his freedom to return to the South and teach other slaves to read and write.*

Paulsen, Gary. *Sarny, a Life Remembered*. New York: Delacorte Press, 1997. *This novel tells the story of a recently freed young black woman who travels through the South searching for her children after the end of the Civil War.*

Paulsen, Gary. *Soldier's Heart*. New York: Delacorte Press, 1998. *Based on the actual experiences of a fifteen-year-old boy who fought for the Union army, this novel shows the horror of combat and its emotional impact on soldiers.*

Reeder, Carolyn. *Across the Lines*. New York: Atheneum Books for Young Readers, 1997. *A novel that tells the parallel stories of twelve-year-old Edward, whose family must leave its plantation in the South during the Civil War, and his slave Simon, who escapes and joins the Union army.*

Reeder, Carolyn. *Shades of Gray*. New York, London: Collier Macmillan, 1989. *In this novel, a twelve-year-old Virginia boy loses his family during the Civil War and goes to live with his uncle, who is considered a traitor by some people because he refused to fight for the Confederate cause.*

Rinaldi, Ann. *Girl in Blue*. New York: Scholastic, 2001. *In this novel, a sixteen-year-old Northern girl pretends to be a man and becomes a spy for the Union army.*

Rinaldi, Ann. *In My Father's House*. New York: Scholastic, 1993. *This book follows the course of the Civil War from the perspective of a young Southern girl who is present during two important events in the conflict: the First Battle of Bull Run in 1861 and Confederate general Robert E. Lee's surrender at Appomattox in 1865.*

Robinet, Harriette Gillem. *Forty Acres and Maybe a Mule*. New York: Atheneum Books for Young Readers, 1998. *This novel tells the story of a fictional group of former slaves who briefly have the chance to farm their own land during Reconstruction.*

Sharra, Jeff. *Gods and Generals*. New York: Ballantine Books, 1996. *In this prequel to his father's novel* The Killer Angels, *Sharra follows several major Civil War generals through the battles of Fredericksburg and Chancellorsville.*

Sharra, Michael. *The Killer Angels*. New York: McKay, 1974. *A Pulitzer Prize–winning novel based on real events and characters in the Battle of Gettysburg.*

Stowe, Harriet Beecher. *Uncle Tom's Cabin*. London: J. Cassell, 1852. Multiple subsequent editions. *A novel presenting a vivid picture of the evils of slavery, it convinced countless Northerners to join the abolitionist movement and contributed to the divisions between North and South that led to the Civil War.*

Wisler, G. Clifton. *Red Cap*. New York: Lodestar Books, 1991. *This book tells the true story of a Union drummer boy who is captured by the Confederate army and sent to the Andersonville prison camp.*

Across Five Aprils

Written by Irene Hunt

Across Five Aprils tells about the American Civil War—which stretched across five Aprils, from April 1861 to April 1865—from the perspective of an Illinois farm boy, Jethro Creighton. Jethro stays at home and works on his family's farm while his brothers go off to fight in the war. He grows up quickly as he follows the conflict through letters and newspaper articles.

Author Irene Hunt based the novel on stories she heard from her grandfather, who actually grew up on an Illinois farm during the Civil War. She also did extensive research to provide accurate information about battles and about the experiences of soldiers. Across Five Aprils won many awards, including the American Notable Book Award, the Clara Ingram Judson Award, and the Lewis Carroll Shelf Award. It was also selected as the runner-up for the prestigious (highly respected) Newbery Medal in 1965.

Biography of author Irene Hunt

Irene Hunt was born on May 18, 1907, in Pontiac, Illinois. Her family moved to Newton, a small town in the south-

Irene Hunt, author of *Across Five Aprils*. *Reproduced by permission of the American Library Association.*

western corner of the state, when she was a baby. Her father, Franklin Pierce Hunt, died when she was seven years old. At that time, she moved to her grandparents' farm with her mother, Sara Land Hunt. Hunt became very close to her grandfather over the years. He had grown up during the Civil War and often shared stories of his experiences with her.

Hunt's grandfather "was a boy of nine at the beginning of the Civil War, and by the time his grandchildren knew him, most of his days were spent in reliving the war years, in which the great struggle sharply touched him and every member of his family," Hunt explained in the author's note for *Across Five Aprils*. "He was a good storyteller, and he gave his listeners a wealth of detail that enabled us to share with him the anxiety and sorrow of the times as well as the moments of happiness in a closely knit family."

Hunt was interested in writing from an early age. "The wish to write pages full of words, to make them tell the stories that I dreamed about, haunted me from childhood on," she noted in the *Dictionary of Literary Biography*. Instead of becoming a writer, however, Hunt spent many years as a schoolteacher. Beginning in 1930, she taught English and French for fifteen years in the Chicago suburb of Oak Park, Illinois. She also worked as a teacher and as a director of language arts in Cicero, Illinois, from 1950 to 1969. In the meantime, she earned a bachelor's degree from the University of Illinois in 1939 and a master's degree from the University of Minnesota in 1946.

During her career as a teacher, Hunt came to believe that interesting, exciting stories could help bring history alive for students. "I felt that teaching history through literature was a happier, more effective process," she said in the *Dictionary of Literary Biography*. But Hunt discovered that it was hard to find good historical fiction for young people. So she decided to try writing these types of books herself. She used her family history and her own experiences to create a realistic picture of life in America during difficult times in history.

Hunt published her first book, *Across Five Aprils,* in 1964. This novel for young adults is based on the stories her grandfather told her about growing up during the Civil War. It tells the story of Jethro Creighton, who is nine years old when the war begins in 1861. He grows up quickly over the next four years as the war affects him and his family. *Across Five Aprils* won several awards and was runner-up for the prestigious Newbery Medal in 1965.

Hunt won the 1967 Newbery Medal for her second book, *Up a Road Slowly.* This novel is based on her own experiences of growing up with only one parent. Hunt retired from teaching in 1969 in order to dedicate herself to writing full-time. She wrote several more works of historical fiction for young people over the years. *No Promises in the Wind,* published in 1970, is about two brothers struggling to survive during the Great Depression of the 1930s. Hunt's 1980 book, *Claws of a Young Century,* focuses on the fight for women's suffrage (the right to vote) in the early 1900s. She published her eighth and final book in 1985. She died in Sayoy, Illinois, on May 18, 2001, at the age of 94.

Historical background of *Across Five Aprils*

Although Jethro Creighton did not really exist, most of the events Hunt describes in *Across Five Aprils* are based on actual events. The author did a great deal of research before writing the novel. She consulted a variety of books and periodicals in order to provide accurate accounts of the major battles of the Civil War. She also used family letters and records in order to present a clear picture of farm life in Illinois in the 1860s. Hunt based the story of the Creighton family on the stories her grandfather told her about growing up during the Civil War.

The novel opens in April 1861. At this time, many Americans were concerned about the hostility and tension that was building between the nation's Northern and Southern regions. The two sides—the North and the South—had become angry and frustrated with each other over several emotional issues, including slavery and the concept of states' rights. Many Northerners believed that slavery was wrong and wanted to abolish (put an end to) it. They also believed that the federal government had the authority to pass laws that applied to all citizens of the United States.

But the economy of the South had been built on slavery, and many Southerners resented Northern efforts to halt or contain the practice. In addition, they argued that the federal government did not have the constitutional power to institute national laws on slavery or anything else. Fearful that the national government might pass laws that would interfere with their traditional way of life, white Southerners argued that each state should decide for itself whether to allow slavery.

In late 1860 and early 1861, a number of Southern states became so angry that they finally followed through on their long-time threat to secede (withdraw) from the United States. These states announced that they would form a new country that allowed slavery, called the Confederate States of America, or the Confederacy. But the U.S. government declared that those states had no right to secede from the Union. Northern political leaders announced that they were willing to use force to keep the nation together. In April 1861, the two sides finally went to war over their differences.

At the time the Civil War began, some Americans faced a difficult decision in choosing which side to support. This was particularly true in the geographic border states of Missouri, Tennessee, Kentucky, Virginia, and Maryland. These states were located in the middle of the country, between the North and the South. In *Across Five Aprils,* Jethro Creighton's family lives in southwestern Illinois. Although Illinois did not allow slavery, it shared its southern border with two slave states, Missouri and Kentucky. Many residents of southern Illinois were born in these states or had relatives there; Jethro's mother, for instance, was born in Kentucky in the novel. In addition, many farmers in this region felt stronger ties to the South, which had an economy based on agriculture, than to the North with its industrial economy.

Illinois voted to remain part of the Union when the Southern states seceded. But not all residents agreed with the majority decision. Some people, like Jethro's brother Bill in the novel, did not think that the national government should use force to bring the Southern states back into the Union. Other people held the racist view that black people were inferior to whites. These people did not have any interest in fighting to free slaves or to improve the lives of black Americans. But many residents of Illinois, like Jethro's father, Matt, did not

During the Civil War era, communication between soldiers and their families was limited to an exchange of letters. Here, a soldier receives news from home. *Pencil drawing by Edwin Forbes. Courtesy of the Library of Congress.*

want to see the United States divided into two or more separate nations. They were willing to fight to preserve the Union. The characters in *Across Five Aprils* argue about all of these issues. Ultimately, Matt Creighton admits that "human nature ain't any better one side of a political line than on the other."

Once the Civil War got started, nearly two hundred thousand Illinois men joined the Union army. Many of these men left their homes, families, and jobs to become soldiers. In *Across Five Aprils,* Jethro's brother John leaves his wife and two sons behind when he joins the army. Similarly, the Creighton family's friend Shadrach Yale leaves his job as a schoolteacher. With all the able-bodied young men off fighting the Confederates, women and children were forced to take on new responsibilities on the home front. For example, Jethro must learn to operate the plow alone and must take the family's wagon into town for supplies.

Finally, the Civil War took an emotional toll on the families of soldiers. Women and children who stayed at home

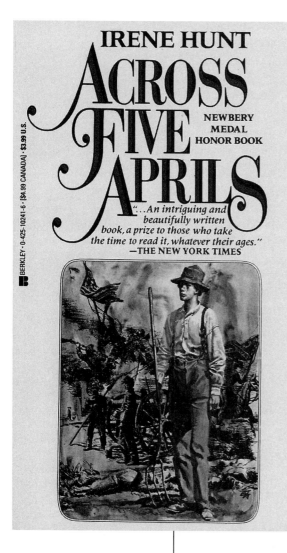

Cover of *Across Five Aprils.*
Reproduced by permission of Penguin Putnam Inc.

spent a great deal of time worrying about their loved ones fighting in distant battles. Letters were usually the only form of communication between soldiers and their families. Jethro's family sends someone to the post office every day in hopes of receiving a letter from one of the brothers serving in the army. The letters they receive provide reassurance that their loved ones are alive and also include vivid descriptions of army life and various battles.

Plot and characters of *Across Five Aprils*

The action in *Across Five Aprils* covers the entire period of the Civil War, from April 1861 to April 1865. As the story begins, nine-year-old Jethro Creighton is planting potatoes with his mother, Ellen, on their family's farm in southern Illinois. They talk about the political situation in the United States at that time, and they wonder whether war will soon begin between the North and the South. Jethro finds the idea of war romantic and exciting. He thinks the North would win any contest in a matter of weeks. He is surprised that his mother views the situation with sadness and dread.

As Jethro thinks about a possible war, his mind drifts to the death of his sister Mary a few years earlier. Mary was on her way home from a dance with her boyfriend when some other boys scared their team of horses. Their wagon overturned and Mary was killed. Some neighbors wanted to take revenge on Travis Burdow, the boy they held responsible for the terrible accident. But Jethro's father, Matt Creighton, convinced the angry mob not to harm the boy.

Jethro is not sure his father made the right decision. He compares his feelings about his father with his feelings about

President Abraham Lincoln (1809–1865), who was still trying to maintain peace with the South. "He had great confidence in his father, but his sense of justice was hard put to accept the fact that Travis Burdow had been allowed to escape the consequences of his drunken crime," Hunt wrote in *Across Five Aprils*. "It occurred to him that he felt the same way toward his father as he did toward Abraham Lincoln—why should the President waver so long? Why should he refuse, week after week, to start the great explosion which the young men wanted to get started and have finished before the year was well into summer?"

As Jethro continues his work, his older cousin, Wilse Graham, arrives unexpectedly from Kentucky for a visit. Over dinner that night, Jethro's family gets into a debate about secession, slavery, and the other issues that seemed to be leading the country toward war. Most of his family supports the position of the North, including his father; his married twenty-four-year-old brother, John; his eighteen-year-old brother, Tom; and his eighteen-year-old cousin, Eb Carron. Wilse Graham argues the position of the South. Jethro's favorite brother, twenty-three-year-old Bill, has points of disagreement with both sides.

Jethro's father, Matt Creighton, says that he is against secession because dividing the United States into two separate countries would make it weak and vulnerable. Brother John Creighton says that slavery is wrong and that the South should not be allowed to spread the practice to new states and territories. But cousin Wilse Graham argues that the Northern half of the country has grown rich at the expense of the Southern half. He says that people in the South just want to continue their way of life without interference from the North. He points out that racism also exists in the North, even without slavery. He says that the Northern abolitionists who wanted to outlaw slavery would be unlikely to welcome blacks into their homes, churches, and schools. "If tomorrow every slave in the South had his freedom and come up North," he asks, "would yore abolitionists git the crocodile tears sloshed out of their eyes so they could take the black man by the hand?"

Later that night, Shadrach Yale, Jethro's schoolteacher and the boyfriend of his sister Jenny, brings news that the Civil War has begun. At first, Jethro is excited and believes that the war will end quickly in a victory for the North. As the

The "War between Brothers"

The Civil War is sometimes called the "war between brothers" because it set people from the same country against each other on the field of battle. It also divided countless communities and families, especially in the geographic border states of Missouri, Tennessee, Kentucky, Virginia, and Maryland. These states were located in the middle of the country, between the North and the South. Although the state governments generally supported slavery, many residents held strong pro-Union feelings. When the war started, many people were forced to choose sides.

"Throughout the border and middle states, tragic scenes took place as families were split, in many cases never to be reunited," James Stokesbury wrote in *A Short History of the Civil War*. "For what we consider as entities—this state or that state—were in reality thousands of agonizing individual choices, as men and women argued and prayed to discover their rightful path and place."

In *Across Five Aprils,* Jethro Creighton and his family live in southwestern Illinois,

just across the border from the slaveholding states of Kentucky and Missouri. Although they oppose slavery, they have relatives in these states and also have a great deal in common with the farmers of the South. After considering all the arguments on both sides, Jethro's favorite brother, Bill, decides that he cannot fight for the Union. Instead, he leaves home and joins the Confederate army. In the meantime, two other Creighton brothers volunteer to fight for the North.

When the Civil War began, many American men were forced to make tough decisions about which side to support. No matter what their decision, it had the potential to tear their families apart. One of the most famous examples is of the family of Mary Todd Lincoln (1818–1882), the wife of President Abraham Lincoln, who led the North during the Civil War. Four of Mrs. Lincoln's brothers fought for the South. Senator John J. Crittenden (1786–1863) of Kentucky faced an even tougher situation. One of his sons became a general in the Union army, and another held the same rank in the Confederate army.

Union army suffers a series of embarrassing defeats over the summer, however, Jethro is forced to realize that the conflict might last a while. His brother Tom and cousin Eb volunteer to join the Union army and leave as soon as they can be spared on the farm. His brother John plans to fight for the North as well. But his brother Bill struggles to decide which side to support.

Bill opposes slavery and does not want the country to
be divided. But he still feels that he has more in common with
the farmers of the South than with the factory owners of the
North. He says that neither side is completely without blame
in the conflict. "I hate slavery, Jeth, but I hate another slavery
of people workin' their lives away in dirty fact'ries fer a wage
that kin scarce keep life in 'em," he explains to his brother. "I
hate secession, but at the same time I can't see how a whole
region kin be able to live if their way of life is all of a sudden
upset." After getting into a fistfight with John over the matter,
Bill leaves home that fall. He tells Jethro that he plans to join
the Confederate army.

As the novel continues, Jethro follows the progress of
the Civil War carefully. He reads articles in the newspaper and
compares the reports with those he receives in letters from his
brothers and Shadrach Yale. He finds the site of each battle on
maps of the United States and tries to see how the results fit
into the strategy of each side. In early 1862, Tom and Eb help

the Union army capture Fort Donelson and Fort Henry in western Kentucky. These forts guard two rivers that provide access deep into Southern territory. Their capture marks an important early victory for the Union. But the boys' letters home show that they no longer consider war glorious and exciting. Instead, they talk about being cold and tired and frightened.

The war also affects Jethro and his family at home. While their brothers are away, Jethro and his sister Jenny must do extra work on the farm and cannot attend school. One day, Jethro's parents send him on an important errand. He takes the family's wagon into the nearest town, Newton, to buy supplies. While there, he is confronted by several men who ask about his brother Bill. The men know that Bill felt sympathetic toward the South and suspect that he joined the Confederate army. Bill's choice makes them very angry, and they target the whole Creighton family for revenge. As Jethro makes the long trip home, the men try to run his wagon off the road. But he is saved by Dave Burdow, the father of the boy who was responsible for the death of Jethro's sister Mary.

The Creighton family expects more trouble and waits anxiously. The stress of worrying about his sons in the war and his family at home causes Matt Creighton to have a heart attack. He lives through it, but he seems older and weaker from that time on. This increases the burden on young Jethro. "If someone had asked Jethro to name a time when he left childhood behind him, he might have named that last week of March in 1862," Hunt wrote in *Across Five Aprils*. "He had learned a great deal about men and their unpredictable behavior the day he drove alone to Newton; now he was to learn what it meant to be the man of a family at ten." One night several weeks later, some men come and burn down the Creightons' barn.

Shortly after their barn is destroyed, the Creighton family learns that Tom has been killed in the Battle of Shiloh in Tennessee. Their friend Ross Milton, editor of the local newspaper, publishes an angry letter to the vandals who destroyed the barn. "May I remind you that Tom Creighton died for the Union cause, that he died in battle, where a man fights his opponent face to face rather than striking and scuttling off into the darkness?" he writes. "And just in passing, Gentlemen, what have you done lately for the Union cause?"

THE SOLDIER'S DREAM OF HOME.

A soldier sleeps, and dreams of better times back home. *Originally published by Currier & Ives. Courtesy of the Library of Congress.*

an irreparable loss." At the end of the book, Jethro learns that Shadrach and Jenny plan to take him back east with them so that he can get a good education.

Style and themes in *Across Five Aprils*

As in her other works of historical fiction, Hunt wrote *Across Five Aprils* in order to help young people understand a difficult time in American history. The author presents several different points of view about the causes of the Civil War. The character Wilse Graham of Kentucky provides a Southern view of the conflict, for example, whereas other members of the Creighton family express the Northern view. Bill Creighton represents the many young men from the border states who had trouble deciding which side to support.

Across Five Aprils covers most of the major events of the Civil War. It begins with the Creighton family getting word that the Confederates have fired on Fort Sumter to start the war. It provides the basic details of every major battle and campaign from that point on. But the focus of the story is Jethro Creighton and his life on the family farm during this time. Jethro does not experience the war directly. Instead, he reads about it in newspaper articles and letters from his brothers, and he hears about it in conversations. Some reviewers compared the structure of Hunt's novel with the tragic plays and stories of ancient Greece. In Greek tragedy, the main characters often hear about or talk about the action of the story rather than participate in it directly. Even though Jethro does not fight in any battles, the story in *Across Five Aprils* moves quickly and provides enough excitement to keep readers' attention.

Although *Across Five Aprils* touches on many different issues, the main theme of the novel is the effect of the Civil War on a boy who remains at home. At the beginning of the book, Jethro Creighton thinks of the war as an exciting way for young men to prove their bravery. But his feelings change as the war drags on for four long years. As Jethro studies his maps and reads his letters and articles, he learns that war creates hardships for everyone involved.

Jethro's life also changes as a result of the war. With his brothers off fighting, he must take on greater responsibility around the family farm. This responsibility weighs heavily on him and forces him to grow up very quickly. By the end of the book, Jethro has gained a greater understanding of the good and bad sides of people. He has also developed a new appreciation for his family and their close relationship. Finally, Jethro has learned the value of education through his friendship with Ross Milton and Shadrach Yale.

Research and Activity Ideas

1) One of the main themes of *Across Five Aprils* is how the Civil War affected the people who remained at home. Make a list of the various ways in which the war affected Jethro Creighton. How do you think his life would have been different if he had lived in the South during the war?

2) Jethro is thirteen years old when the Civil War ends, but in some ways he seems much older. How did Jethro grow and change from April 1861 to April 1865? What events in the novel had the greatest influence on his maturity?

3) In Chapter 2 of *Across Five Aprils,* the Creighton family has a heated discussion about some of the issues that led to the Civil War. What are the main disagreements between the North and the South? Outline some of the major points on both sides. If you were one of the Creighton brothers, which side would you support?

4) Throughout *Across Five Aprils,* Jethro follows the events of the Civil War by reading newspaper articles and letters from his brothers. He often looks at maps of the areas where battles take place and tries to figure out the strategy of each side. Choose a major battle of the Civil War and read several accounts of it, including at least one written by a participant. Locate the battle site on a map and use the accounts you read to re-create what happened.

5) During the Civil War, people in both the North and the South were accused of secretly supporting the other side. When this sort of suspicion got out of hand, it sometimes led to intimidation and violence. An example occurs in *Across Five Aprils,* when some neighbors burn down the Creightons' barn because one of their sons favors the Confederacy. During World War II (1939–45), thousands of Americans of Japanese descent were forcibly removed from their homes and placed in internment camps, even though they were loyal to the United States in its war against Japan. How is what happened to the Creightons similar to the treatment received by Japanese Americans during World War II?

Related Titles

Beatty, Patricia. *Jayhawker.* New York: Morrow Junior Books, 1991. *In this novel, a Kansas teenager who opposes slavery becomes a "Jayhawker"—an abolitionist raider who sets slaves free—and faces danger from his neighbors.*

Burns, Ken, director. *The Civil War.* Walpole, NH: Florentine Films/PBS, 1990. *This nine-part documentary film series tells the story of the Civil War through letters, photographs, and newspaper articles.*

Reeder, Carolyn. *Shades of Gray.* New York: Macmillan, 1989. *In this novel, a twelve-year-old Virginia boy loses his family during the Civil War and goes to live with his uncle, who is considered a traitor by some people because he refused to fight for the Confederate cause.*

Shenandoah. Universal, 1965. *This film stars James Stewart as a Virginia farmer who tries to remain neutral during the Civil War while members of his family take sides.*

Where to Learn More About . . .

Irene Hunt and *Across Five Aprils*

"Across Five Aprils." In *Literature and Its Times*. Vol. 2. Detroit: Gale, 1998.

Beem, Wendell Bruce. "Aunt Irene." *Horn Book*. August 1967.

"Irene Hunt" in *Contemporary Authors, New Revision Series*. Vol. 57. Detroit: Gale, 1997.

Sadler, Philip A. "Irene Hunt." In *Dictionary of Literary Biography*. Vol. 52 *American Writers for Children since 1960*. Detroit: Gale, 1986.

The Experiences of Soldiers and Civilians in the Civil War

Hicken, Victor. *Illinois in the Civil War*. Chicago: University of Illinois Press, 1991.

McPherson, James M. *What They Fought For: 1861–1865*. Baton Rouge: Louisiana State University Press, 1994.

Stokesbury, James. *A Short History of the Civil War*. New York: W. Morrow, 1995.

Tapert, Annette, ed. *The Brothers' War: Civil War Letters to Their Loved Ones from the Blue and Gray*. New York: Random House, 1988.

Forty Acres and Maybe a Mule

Written by Harriette Gillem Robinet

Forty Acres and Maybe a Mule takes place immediately after the end of the American Civil War (1861–65), during the period in American history known as Reconstruction (1865–77). During this time, the U.S. government introduced several programs designed to help the millions of African American slaves who had gained their freedom during the war. One of these programs involved giving land to former slaves so that they could grow crops and support their families. Sadly, this program ended only a few months after it began, and most of the slaves who had received land were forced to give it up.

In *Forty Acres and Maybe a Mule,* Harriette Gillem Robinet tells the story of a fictional group of former slaves who briefly have the chance to farm their own land. She shows the hope and disappointment of the Reconstruction era through the eyes of a twelve-year-old black boy named Pascal. Her novel won the Scott O'Dell Award for Historical Fiction in 1998.

Biography of author Harriette Gillem Robinet

Harriette Gillem Robinet was born on July 14, 1931, in Washington, D.C. Her parents, Richard and Martha Gillem, were

**Harriette Gillem Robinet,
author of _Forty Acres
and Maybe a Mule._**
_Photograph by McLouis
Robinet. Reproduced by
permission of Harriette Robinet._

both teachers. Robinet developed an interest in the history of slavery in the United States at an early age. Her interest was fueled by her family history: Her maternal grandparents had been slaves on the estate of the Confederate general Robert E. Lee (1807–1870) in Arlington, Virginia, before the Civil War.

Robinet earned a bachelor's degree from the College of New Rochelle (New York) in 1953. She later completed master's and doctorate degrees in microbiology at the Catholic University of America in Washington, D.C. Robinet worked for many years as a bacteriologist (a scientist who studies bacteria) and also taught biology. In 1960, she married McLouis Robinet. They eventually had six children together.

One of Robinet's sons has cerebral palsy. His struggles to overcome physical and emotional obstacles inspired her to write about disabled children. Robinet published her first children's book, _Jay and the Marigold,_ in 1976. It tells the story of a handicapped boy who is treated as an outsider in school until he becomes friends with a new student.

Robinet has also written several historical novels for young people, including _Children of the Fire_ (1991) and _The Twins, the Pirates, and the Battle of New Orleans_ (1997). She drew upon her interest in slavery when writing _Forty Acres and Maybe a Mule,_ which was published in 1998. Although Robinet had heard many stories about slavery, she realized that she did not know much about Reconstruction. She researched the experiences of African Americans during this period in history and wrote a story about it. Robinet lives with her husband in Oak Park, Illinois.

Historical background of _Forty Acres and Maybe a Mule_

Robinet created the characters in _Forty Acres and Maybe a Mule_ in her imagination. The story, however, takes place against the background of real events that happened during Reconstruction.

When the North won the Civil War in April 1865, the practice of slavery ended throughout the country. The Union victory also established the fact that states were not allowed to secede (withdraw) from the United States. But the end of the war also raised a whole new set of questions. For example, American political leaders had to decide whether to punish the Southern states for their rebellion. They also had to set up a process through which the Confederate states could rejoin the Union. Finally, they had to decide how much help the government should provide the newly freed slaves. The period in American history when the country struggled to settle these complicated issues is known as Reconstruction. It was a time of great political and social turmoil.

President Andrew Johnson (1808–1875), who took office after President Abraham Lincoln (1809–1865) was assassinated, took charge of the early Reconstruction efforts. Johnson pardoned (officially forgave) many former Confederates and established simple rules for the Southern states to rejoin the Union. But many people in the North felt that the president was too easy on the South. Within a short time, several Southern states elected former Confederate leaders to represent them in the U.S. Congress. It also became clear that most white Southerners had no interest in granting black people equal rights as citizens. Instead, they passed a series of harsh laws known as the Black Codes that restricted the activities of blacks and ensured that whites maintained power over them. For example, black people were not allowed to own weapons, testify in court, or buy land in certain areas. In addition, the laws said that homeless blacks could be leased out to work for whites against their will. The Black Codes returned African Americans to a condition close to slavery in Southern society.

As former Confederates returned to power and discrimination against blacks continued in the South, many people in the North became angry. They wondered why they had fought in the Civil War if doing so had not changed anything in the South. After bitter arguments with Johnson, the U.S. Congress decided to take over responsibility for Reconstruction.

First, Congress passed the Civil Rights Act of 1866, which made most provisions of the Black Codes illegal. Then, in

March 1867, Congress passed the Reconstruction Act. This act separated the defeated Southern states into five military districts and sent federal troops to maintain order in each one. It also required each state to hold a convention to rewrite the basic laws in its constitution. All adult men, black or white, were allowed to vote and participate in the conventions. Black men jumped at the chance to have a say in their state governments. In general, the conventions produced state constitutions that were more fair for all citizens. For example, they guaranteed equal rights for whites and blacks, increased assistance to the poor, and created public school systems that were open to both races, although schools were still segregated. Congress also established two amendments to the U.S. Constitution. The Fourteenth Amendment granted the rights of citizenship to former slaves and protected them against discrimination. The Fifteenth Amendment prevented states from restricting the right of black men to vote.

Most of the Southern states were allowed to rejoin the United States in 1868. Many Southern whites continued to believe that blacks were inferior and did not deserve equal rights. Violence broke out across the South as angry whites rebelled against the Reconstruction policies and the new state governments. Some people—known as "white supremacists," owing to their belief that blacks were inferior—used violence to intimidate blacks and to prevent them from using their new rights. For example, they bombed or set fire to black schools and churches, and they terrorized blacks who held public office, owned businesses, or operated successful farms. Over time, this violence and intimidation gradually returned political power in the South to whites.

Reconstruction officially ended in 1877, when President Rutherford B. Hayes (1822–1893) withdrew federal troops from the South. From this time onward, the North left the South to settle its own racial issues. Unfortunately, many issues remained unresolved for generations. Although slavery was illegal, discrimination against blacks continued in much of the South. In the end, Reconstruction failed to ensure equal rights for African Americans. The government forced the southern states to give blacks greater political and legal rights but stopped short of providing former slaves with land, education, and jobs. Without these necessities, black people never had a chance to make other changes permanent.

Still, Reconstruction was not a complete failure. For a brief time, it had offered African Americans broad new rights and opportunities. Black men gained the right to vote and were elected to office. Many slave families were reunited. Some former slaves managed to save enough money to buy homes and open businesses. It also set the stage for the civil rights movement that would take place nearly one hundred years later. Reconstruction "remained in the memories of Negroes [African Americans] and a minority of whites," Allen W. Trelease explained in *Reconstruction: The Great Experiment.* "They might be outnumbered and silenced for the present, but they would not always be. When the same dedication to equal rights arose in a later day, Reconstruction remained as a precedent and stimulus to further progress."

Land for freed slaves. One of the most difficult problems during Reconstruction involved helping four million newly freed slaves build independent lives for themselves. Many former slaves believed that true freedom meant owning land. With their own land, they could grow crops to feed their families. This way, they could support themselves and not depend on plantation owners.

Black people first began receiving land from the U.S. government before the end of the Civil War, in January 1865. At this time, Union general William T. Sherman (1820–1891) issued Field Order 15, which provided forty acres of land to each family of freed slaves. Sherman had just completed a march across the state of Georgia with his army. As the Union forces traveled through the South, thousands of slaves ran away from their plantations and followed the army. Sherman issued his unusual order as a way to rid himself of the responsibility of caring for these slaves.

When the war ended a few months later, the U.S. government made Sherman's plan official. They formed a special agency, called the Freedmen's Bureau, to help former slaves get settled and build new lives for themselves. The Freedmen's Bureau provided food, clothing, and other assistance to the freed slaves until they could support themselves. It also set up hospitals, orphanages, and thousands of schools to help blacks and poor whites in the South.

In the spring of 1865, the Freedmen's Bureau began issuing forty acres of land to former slave families. About forty

Union general William T. Sherman. *Photograph by Mathew Brady. Courtesy of the Library of Congress.*

thousand African Americans took advantage of the program and started farming their own land. But in September of that year, another government ruling took the land back from black families. Only about fifteen hundred former slaves managed to keep their land, mostly those who lived on the sea islands off the coast of Georgia and South Carolina. The characters in *Forty Acres and Maybe a Mule* receive the title to forty acres of "Sherman lands" in the spring of 1865, create a working farm, and then lose their property in September of that year.

Plot and characters of *Forty Acres and Maybe a Mule*

The story in *Forty Acres and Maybe a Mule* begins in April 1865, just after the end of the Civil War. The main character in the novel is Pascal, a twelve-year-old African American boy who is a slave on a plantation in South Carolina. Pascal's arm and leg are deformed, so he works as a servant in the master's house rather than in the cotton fields. As the story begins, Pascal feels very lonely. His father and four of his brothers were sold away from the plantation years earlier. His older brother, Gideon, ran away two years earlier to join the Union army. His mother, Jerusalem City, was shot and killed by the overseer the previous winter because she asked for more food for the starving slaves.

Pascal is thrilled when Gideon shows up unexpectedly one night. Gideon tells his brother that the war is over and the North won. He says that this means slavery is illegal and they are now free. Gideon also tells Pascal about an order issued by Union general William T. Sherman that offered forty acres and maybe a mule to former slave families who want to start their own farms. Gideon asks Pascal to come with him to Georgia to claim a plot of land. Before they leave, Pascal invites his friend Nelly, an eight-year-old girl who is also a slave on the plantation, to join them.

The three young people travel for several weeks. Along the way to Georgia, Pascal sees hundreds of former slaves on the roads. Many blacks are looking for family members who were sold away from them under slavery. Others are hoping to find paying jobs. Pascal also sees homes and farms that have suffered damage during the war. "Southern white folks be plenty angry

Cover of *Forty Acres and Maybe a Mule*. *Jacket illustration © 1998 by Bessie Nickens. Reproduced by permission of Bessie Nickens.*

at the North," he observes. "President Lincoln's trying, but this freedom ain't gonna be that easy." Each time they reach a town, Gideon asks whether it has offices of the Freedmen's Bureau—a government agency that handled the distribution of land to freed slaves and poor white people. But each time, they fail to find an office and must continue down the road.

Whenever horses or wagons approach, the three travelers and all the other former slaves walking along the road run into the woods to hide. Even though they know they are free, they are still afraid that their masters will capture them and return them to slavery. At one point, Pascal sees an elderly black man who refuses to hide and keeps walking down the road. A white man in a wagon tells him to return to his master. But the old man says that he is free and no one owns him. In fact, he declares that his name is Mr. Freedman. In response, the angry white man pulls out a pistol and shoots at him. The old man falls to the ground, and the white man drives away in his wagon. Pascal and his companions are horrified and rush to help the old man. But when the young people approach, they find that he is not hurt. The bullet fired by the white man had missed. Mr. Freedman stands up, and he travels with them from that time on.

As they walk along, the four former slaves debate the meaning of freedom. Mr. Freedman says that freedom is about having dignity, while Gideon argues that freedom is about owning land. Nelly describes freedom as a certain way a person feels inside. Pascal has trouble putting his ideas into words and finally decides that freedom must mean different things to different people. He also wonders whether they are truly free since they must hide from angry, racist whites. "Sure, they were free. But if nobody allowed their freedom, what would owning land mean?" Pascal thinks to himself. "This kind of freedom was as bad as slavery."

After about two weeks on the road, Pascal and his companions camp one night with a large group of other freed slaves. They all hide when a wagon approaches on the road above. Two horsemen gallop up to the wagon and ask the white family inside whether they have seen any runaway slaves. The riders explain that they plan to capture black people and force them to return to work in their fields. The father claims that they have not seen anyone on the road. Then the

mother asks the men whether they plan to pay the black people for their work now that they are free. "We ain't about to pay Negroes to work when we own them in the first place, and we can whip them into working without wages in the second place," replies one of the riders.

After the men leave, the family brings their wagon to where the black people had been camped. The family's daughter, twelve-year-old Judith Bibb, finds Pascal in his hiding place and introduces him to her family. The Bibbs are poor Baptists who were forced to leave their home in Tennessee during the war. Like Gideon, they are hoping to claim forty acres of land and start a new life. The other black people slowly emerge from their hiding places as they learn that the Bibbs mean them no harm. Pascal and Nelly make friends with Judith and her six-year-old brother, Matthew.

A few days later, Gideon finally finds an office of the Freedmen's Bureau in the small town of River Stop, Georgia. By this time, their group has expanded to include Mr. Freedman's granddaughter, Gladness, who is a pretty girl about Gideon's age. The five former slaves present themselves as a family and receive tools, seeds, and the title to forty acres of land. Pascal and Gideon decide to use the last name City as a tribute to their mother, Jerusalem City. Nelly adopts this name as well. While they are in town, Pascal and Nelly drop by a school that has been established by the Freedmen's Bureau. While they are there, some men on horseback shoot their guns through the windows of the school. Everyone is frightened but unhurt, and the children are determined to attend school anyway.

When they locate their land, Pascal and his companions are thrilled to find that it features a lake, a stream, and a twisted old oak known as a "ghost tree." The Bibbs' property is just across the lake. Gideon hires several other former slaves who are passing by on the road. Within a short time, they burn off the grass, plant a cotton crop and a food garden, build a small farmhouse, and dig a well. They soon have a model farm. Pascal and Nelly attend school and learn to read and write. Gideon and Mr. Freedman register to vote. Thanks to Reconstruction, Pascal feels like a person who is worthy of respect for the first time in his life.

But Pascal also worries about the constant threat to their freedom. He knows that many white people in the

South are angry about the outcome of the war and refuse to accept the end of slavery. They are determined to maintain their power in society and prevent blacks from gaining equal rights. Some of these people resort to violence in order to intimidate black people. For example, they burn down a nearby black settlement called Jubilee Town, and they kill a black neighbor who ran his own cattle ranch. Concerned that a successful black-owned farm might be a target for such people, Pascal arranges for his white friends Judith and Matthew to play near their farmhouse so people passing by think it is owned by whites.

One day, all the former slaves are called to a meeting in River Stop. The man who runs the Freedmen's Bureau warns them about the Black Codes—new state laws that say that any black people found wandering the roads can be arrested and forced to work on a plantation. To avoid the Black Codes, all the people who work on the City family farm have to sign work contracts proving that they have a paying job. Otherwise they will be considered "vagrants." Pascal is horrified when several black people who attend the meeting are arrested and taken away. "Freed slaves were losing their freedom," he notes. "Little by little they must have felt good about themselves that summer; now they were back to working like slaves. No, worse than slaves: They were being arrested and had to work out their fines like prisoners. This was wrong, wrong, wrong."

Late in the summer, Gideon finds a bag of gold coins hidden under the roots of the ghost tree. He gives a few coins to each of the people who have helped work the farm. As autumn approaches, Gideon and Gladness get married. But their happiness is checked by their constant worry about losing the farm. "I feel it only be a matter of time," Gideon says. "Time till I lose my farm. Just a few of us colored that ain't been shot at, or burned out, or scared away. It be just a matter of time." As Pascal thinks back on all of the negative and frightening things that have happened since he left the plantation, he wonders, "What kind of freedom was this? Why couldn't white people just let them live?"

In September, a white man visits their farm with a representative of the Freedmen's Bureau. He immediately takes notice of the neatly planted, insect-free crops, the lake and

creek for irrigation, and the sturdy house. He tells the man from the Freedmen's Bureau that he plans to claim the land and force the black people to work for him. "The Southern farmers have caught the ear of President Johnson, it seems," the man from the Freedmen's Bureau explains. "They're suffering from crops poorly planted and no workers for picking. They lived for two hundred years on slave labor, and now they're suffering. They want former slaves to return to their plantation fields. Circular Fifteen says Sherman Lands are only available to white people. All former slaves must give up their lands."

The new owner of the farm comes over to Pascal and asks his name. But with his new confidence and sense of self-worth, Pascal refuses to answer. Through his defiance, he learns what freedom means to him. "In keeping silent, not doing what the man asked, he felt triumphant," Robinet writes. "It was the first time in his whole life that he hadn't obeyed a white man. The defiance, the triumph, was this what Mama felt? Was this what Gideon felt? Something surged inside him, some new feeling. Freedom? Yes! He felt strong and black and free. He was somebody. . . . HE WAS SOME-BODY, AND ALWAYS HAD BEEN. Was that what Mama had known? She had asked for food for dying slaves. Maybe Mama had known freedom after all! Master may have owned her work, but her spirit was free! Maybe nobody gave freedom, and nobody could take it away like they could take away a family farm. Maybe freedom was something you claimed for yourself."

That night, all of the former slaves take apart the farmhouse and move it to the Bibbs' property. They also fill in the well so the white man cannot use it. Then they sadly go their separate ways. Pascal, Nelly, Gideon, and Gladness plan to head toward the Atlantic coast of Georgia, where they have heard that land is still available to former slave families on the sea islands. Although Pascal is sad about the loss of their farm, and angry about being treated unfairly, he remains hopeful about beginning a new life. "Inside him surged a wave of dignity. He was somebody even without land!" Robinet explains. "He was free, and nothing—lame leg, weak arm, family farm taken away, torn pants—nothing else mattered. Inside him blossomed the freedom that had been growing. It seemed to burst his chest. He promised himself to never let it go."

Style and themes in *Forty Acres and Maybe a Mule*

Robinet wrote the story of Pascal and his makeshift family in the third person. In a third-person narrative, an observer (rather than a character) describes the events in the book and the emotions of the characters to the reader. This style of writing allows the narrator to remain outside of the action. In this way, readers can evaluate the events in the book and form their own opinions.

One of the main themes of *Forty Acres and Maybe a Mule* involves the positive and negative experiences of former slaves during Reconstruction. Pascal, Gideon, and their friends feel great joy about finally gaining their freedom. They work hard to get land of their own and build a successful farm, and they are proud of the results of their efforts. But their feelings of happiness and pride are always mixed with feelings of anxiety and fear. After all, they know that many white people in the South are angry that the U.S. government has freed the slaves. These white people want black people to continue to work for them without pay, and they resent former slaves who insist that they be treated as equals. Pascal sees many examples of angry white people lashing out with violence against blacks. He knows that their successful, black-owned family farm is in constant danger from such people. So while Pascal sees the possibilities of freedom, he also recognizes that—for now, at least—his freedom also has limits.

Pascal's mixture of positive and negative experiences reflects the overall experiences of freed slaves during Reconstruction. Many slaves welcomed freedom with excitement and hope. They dreamed of building new, independent lives for themselves and their families. At first, it appeared as if the government's policies would enable blacks to gain equal rights in American society. But before long, the former slaves began to see their new rights and opportunities slip away—just as Pascal and Gideon lost their family farm. Their feelings of hope are mixed with frustration and disappointment.

Another theme in the novel involves the concept of family. At the beginning of the story, all of Pascal's relatives have either died, been sold, or run away from the plantation. He is thrilled when his brother Gideon comes to find him, and throughout their travels he asks the people he meets if they

have any information about his lost brothers. But it soon becomes clear to Pascal that people do not have to be related by blood in order to be a family. He grows very close to Nelly and protects her like a brother. He respects Mr. Freedman and considers him a grandfather. As all the former slaves work together to farm the City land, Pascal realizes that they are all part of a larger family.

Research and Activity Ideas

1) Throughout *Forty Acres and Maybe a Mule,* Pascal struggles to understand the meaning of freedom. Discuss what freedom means to different characters in the book, such as Gideon, Nelly, Mr. Freedman, and Jerusalem City. How does Pascal finally define the term for himself?

2) Pascal and his companions receive the title to forty acres of land and build a successful family farm, only to see their property taken away. Tell the class about a time when something valuable to you was lost or taken away. How did you feel?

3) Reconstruction ultimately failed to provide equal rights for black people in American society. Still, in her author's note for *Forty Acres and Maybe a Mule,* Robinet says that Reconstruction was "a glorious time for freed African Americans." List some of the positive and negative effects of Reconstruction policies on the lives of former slaves.

Related Titles

The Color Purple. Warner Brothers, 1985. *This film follows the struggles of a poor black girl living in a small Georgia town during the first half of the twentieth century.*

Hansen, Joyce. *I Thought My Soul Would Rise and Fly.* New York: Scholastic, 1997. *The fictional diary of a twelve-year-old African American slave girl who gains her freedom at the end of the Civil War.*

McKissack, Patricia C. *A Picture of Freedom: The Diary of Clotee, a Slave Girl, Belmont Plantation.* New York: Scholastic, 1997. *A novel about an African American girl who tries to understand the true meaning of freedom.*

Paulsen, Gary. *Sarny, a Life Remembered.* New York: Delacorte Press, 1997. *This novel tells the story of a recently freed young black woman who travels through the South searching for her children after the end of the Civil War.*

Smith, John D. *Black Voices from Reconstruction*. Brookfield, CT: Millbrook Press, 1996. *A collection of personal accounts of the struggles of former slaves following the end of the Civil War.*

Where to Learn More About . . .

Harriette Gillem Robinet and *Forty Acres and Maybe a Mule*

Contemporary Authors Online. Detroit: Gale, 2001.

Something about the Author. Vol. 27. Detroit: Gale, 1982.

Reconstruction

DuBois, W. E. B. *Black Reconstruction*. New York: Harcourt, 1935. Reprint, New York: Atheneum, 1992.

Foner, Eric. *Reconstruction: America's Unfinished Revolution, 1863–1877*. New York: Harper and Row, 1988.

Franklin, John Hope. *Reconstruction after the Civil War*. Chicago: University of Chicago Press, 1961, 1994.

McPherson, James M. *Ordeal by Fire: The Civil War and Reconstruction*. New York: Knopf, 1982.

Mettger, Zak. *Reconstruction: America After the Civil War*. New York: Lodestar/Dutton, 1994.

Sterling, Dorothy, ed. *The Trouble They Seen: Black People Tell the Story of Reconstruction*. New York: Doubleday, 1976.

Trelease, Allen W. *Reconstruction: The Great Experiment*. New York: Harper and Row, 1971.

In My Father's House

Written by Ann Rinaldi

In My Father's House is based on the true story of Wilmer McLean (1814–1882), a merchant from Virginia who played an unusual role in the American Civil War (1861–65). The first major battle of the war took place on McLean's plantation near Manassas in 1861. Hoping to protect his family from further conflict, McLean bought a farmhouse two hundred miles away in Appomattox County—far enough away, he thought, from any wartime activity. But the war followed him there. In 1865, McLean's home became the site of the historic meeting at which Confederate general Robert E. Lee (1807–1870) surrendered to Union general Ulysses S. Grant (1822–1885). Strange as it may seem, McLean could say that the Civil War began in his front yard and ended in his parlor.

The story in *In My Father's House* centers around McLean's stepdaughter, Oscie Mason. Oscie is seven years old when her mother, Virginia Hooe Mason, marries Wilmer McLean. Oscie has many disagreements with her stepfather over the years. By the time the Civil War ends, however, she has come to admire his determination to support and protect her family.

Ann Rinaldi, author of *In My Father's House*. *Photograph by Bart Ehrenberg. Reproduced by permission of Ann Rinaldi.*

Biography of author Ann Rinaldi

The author of *In My Father's House* is Ann Rinaldi, a well-known writer of historical fiction for young adults. Rinaldi was born on August 27, 1934, in New York City. Her mother died shortly after her birth. At this time, Rinaldi was sent to live with an aunt and uncle in Brooklyn. She was very happy living there. But then her father remarried and brought her back to live with him and her stepmother. From this point on, Rinaldi recalls her childhood as being unhappy. She loved to read and always wanted to be a writer, but her father discouraged her.

"My father did not believe in college for his daughters, so I was sent into the business world to become a secretary," Rinaldi once said in an interview for *Contemporary Authors.* She worked as a typist for several years, until she met and married Ronald Rinaldi in 1960. Her husband gave her the stable, middle-class life she had wanted since childhood. She quit her job and had two children, Ronald Jr. and Marcella. Rinaldi first started trying to write fiction during these years, but she later called her early efforts "terrible."

In 1969, Rinaldi began writing a column for a local newspaper. She then took a job with the *Trentonian* in Trenton, New Jersey, and expanded into writing feature articles. She worked as a journalist for twenty years. She also returned to fiction writing during this time. Rinaldi found that her experiences as a journalist and as a parent gave her plenty of interesting material to write about. She published her first novel for young adults, *Term Paper,* in 1980. This book tells the story of a girl named Nicki who uses a school assignment to come to terms with her feelings about her father's death. Rinaldi published several other contemporary novels over the next few years.

Rinaldi first became interested in writing historical fiction when her children became involved in reenactments (events at which groups of people dress up in costumes and act out events from history) of the American Revolution. She used the Revolutionary War (1775–83) as the subject of several of her books, including *Time Enough for Drums* (1986), *A Ride into Morning* (1991), and *Cast Two Shadows* (1998). She has also published several historical novels set during the Civil War, including *The Last Silk Dress* (1988), *In My Father's House* (1993), *Mine Eyes Have Seen* (1997), and *Amelia's War* (1999).

As the author of more than a dozen works of historical fiction for young adults, Rinaldi is known for her thorough research, interesting plots, and realistic characters. She begins her research in her large, personal library. She also visits public libraries and historic sites and reviews private manuscript collections as she gathers information to write a new book. She bases her books on real people and events and then uses her imagination to fill in the gaps in recorded history. "All historical novelists have to invent much of the motivation of their characters in order to take them from one historically accurate event to the next," she explained in *Something about the Author.*

Many of Rinaldi's novels feature strong girls who grow up and make choices during difficult times in American history. Her books have been praised for making history more interesting for teenagers. In 1991, Rinaldi received a National History Award from the Daughters of the American Revolution for her contributions in "bringing history to life." "I write young adult novels because I like it," she stated in *Something about the Author.* "I have an aim to write good stuff for [teenagers], to treat them as people, not write down to them with stories about romance and acne and the spring dance." Rinaldi lives with her husband in Somerville, New Jersey.

Historical background of *In My Father's House*

The events in *In My Father's House* take place during the Civil War. This was a conflict between the northern part of the United States, known as the Union, and the southern half of the country, known as the Confederacy. For many years before the war began in 1861, the two sides argued bitterly over several issues, including slavery.

Many people in the North believed that slavery was wrong and wanted to outlaw the practice. But the South's economy depended on slavery, and white Southerners argued that the national government should not interfere with their traditional way of life. When it became clear that the two sides could not reach an agreement, several Southern states seceded (withdrew) from the United States and formed their own country that allowed slavery, called the Confederate States of America (or the Confederacy). But Northern political leaders were determined not to let the Southern states leave the Union without a fight.

Rinaldi based *In My Father's House* on the true story of Wilmer McLean and his family. McLean was born on May 3, 1814. He made a living as a merchant in Virginia. He married a widow named Virginia Hooe Mason in 1853 and helped raise her young daughters. When the Civil War began, McLean gave his plantation to the Confederate army. His house became the headquarters of Confederate general Pierre G. T. Beauregard (1818–1893) during the First Battle of Bull Run (also known as the First Battle of Manassas) in July 1861. In fact, this first major battle of the Civil War took place on McLean's property.

The McLean plantation was located in northern Virginia, near the Bull Run River and an important railroad junction called Manassas. As the Civil War began, twenty thousand Confederate troops under Beauregard moved into the area. Union leaders viewed these troops as a threat to Washington, D.C., which was only twenty-five miles away. They also knew that Beauregard's army blocked the path Union forces would have to take in order to capture the Confederate capital of Richmond, Virginia. Finally, Union leaders faced a great deal of pressure to launch an offensive attack, which people in the North felt would bring a quick end to the war. For all these reasons, the Union moved two armies consisting of fifty thousand men toward Manassas in the summer of 1861. People in Washington, D.C., were so certain of a Union victory that hundreds of spectators came to watch the battle.

When the fighting began on July 21, 1861, it soon became clear that troops on both sides were poorly trained and disorganized. In fact, neither side had official uniforms at this early point in the war. As a result, some men on both sides wore the same colors as enemy soldiers, and the confused

The McLean house in Appomattox Court House, Virginia. *Photograph by Timothy H. O'Sullivan. Courtesy of the National Archives and Records Administration.*

armies sometimes ended up firing on their own troops. At one point in the battle, Union forces nearly broke through the Confederate lines at a spot called Henry House Hill. But Confederate forces under General Thomas "Stonewall" Jackson (1824–1863) managed to hold off the attack. Finally, eleven thousand more Confederate troops under General Joseph E. Johnston (1807–1891) arrived by railroad line. With the help of these reinforcements, the Confederates forced the Union troops to make a hasty retreat. The Northern spectators fled back to the safety of Washington. The Confederate victory in the First Battle of Bull Run shocked people in the North and thrilled people in the South. It also convinced both sides that the war was going to be a long and bloody one.

When he realized that a battle was going to take place on his property, Wilmer McLean moved his family out of harm's way. They eventually settled in Appomattox Court House in southern Virginia, about two hundred miles away from their former home. McLean chose this spot because he believed that the war would never reach it. But he never antic-ipated that the war would last for four years and claim the lives of over six hundred thousand Americans.

As the conflict dragged on into 1865, it became clear to most people that the South was going to lose. Union forces had captured most major cities in the South and done a great deal of damage to the land. The Confederate army was run-ning low on food, clothing, ammunition, and other supplies. It seemed to be only a matter of time before the South would be forced to give up.

Even the South's greatest army, the Army of Northern Virginia, led by General Robert E. Lee, showed the scars of four years of warfare. By March 1865, Lee had only fifty thousand troops left, and his men were tired and hungry. Despite their weariness, however, Lee's forces maintained a fierce defense of the Confederate capital of Richmond and the nearby city of Petersburg, Virginia, which contained railroad lines that car-ried supplies to the capital. They faced off against the Union's Army of the Potomac, led by General Ulysses S. Grant. Grant had twice as many men as Lee, with thousands of reinforce-ments on the way.

On April 1, Grant's forces took control of the last rail-way line into Richmond. At this point, the Union general ordered a full assault on the Confederate capital. The follow-ing day, Confederate president Jefferson Davis (1808–1889) and his government evacuated Richmond. On April 3, Lee managed to escape the city and moved his ragged forces across the Appomattox River. With Lee out of the way, Grant quickly took control of both Richmond and Petersburg. Although this was a great victory for the North, Grant knew that the war would not end until Lee surrendered. The Union general believed that if Lee gave up the fight, then other Confederate armies would lay down their arms as well.

Grant followed Lee across the river. By April 8, Union forces had surrounded the Army of Northern Virginia near a small town called Appomattox Court House. Grant sent a mes-sage to his rival, asking him to surrender. One of Lee's officers suggested that he order his soldiers to scatter into the woods and keep up the fight in small groups. But Lee refused to accept this idea. He worried that it would only cause the Union troops to chase the men and destroy more of the South. He regretfully

told his men that he planned to surrender. "There is nothing left for me to do but to go and see General Grant, and I would rather die a thousand deaths," he noted.

On April 9, 1865, Generals Grant and Lee met at Wilmer McLean's farmhouse to discuss terms of surrender (see box). According to witnesses, both men appeared as they are described in Rinaldi's novel. Acting on instructions from President Abraham Lincoln (1809–1965), Grant offered Lee generous terms of surrender. For example, the Union general allowed Confederate soldiers to keep their horses so that they could work their farms and feed their families when they returned home. The agreement eased the pain of the defeated Confederates and made it possible for them to return home with some measure of pride and hope for the future. "In Grant, Lee met a man who was as anxious as himself to see this hardest of wars followed by a good peace," Bruce Catton wrote in *The Civil War*. "Grant believed that the whole point of the war had been the effort to prove that Northerners and Southerners

Confederate general Robert E. Lee (seated, left) signs the terms of surrender in Appomattox Court House, Virginia, ending the Civil War. Union general Ulysses S. Grant (seated, with legs crossed) looks on. *Reproduced by permission of Archive Photos.*

Grant Describes Lee's Surrender

A short time before his death in 1885, Union general Ulysses S. Grant published a book about his life. In *The Personal Memoirs of U. S. Grant,* the general describes his meeting with Confederate general Robert E. Lee at Appomattox Court House, Virginia. Although Grant is excited about the Union victory, he shows tremendous respect for Lee and the Confederate Army of Northern Virginia:

> What General Lee's feelings were I do not know. As he was a man of much dignity, with an impassable [hard to read or expressionless] face, it was impossible to say whether he felt inwardly glad that the end had finally come, or felt sad over the result, and was too manly to show it. Whatever his feelings, they were entirely concealed from my observation; but my own feelings, which had been quite jubilant [happy and excited] on the receipt of his letter [accepting the terms of surrender and agreeing to meet], were sad and depressed. I felt like anything rather than rejoicing at the downfall of a foe who had fought so long and valiantly [bravely], and had suffered so much for a cause, though that cause was, I believe, one of the worst for which a people ever fought, and one for which there was the least excuse. I do not question, however, the sincerity of the great mass of those who were opposed to us. . . .

After the two generals sign a formal agreement outlining the terms of the Confederate surrender, Lee leaves. Grant describes what he did next:

> Lee and I then separated as cordially [in a polite and friendly manner] as we had met, he returning to his own lines, and all went into bivouac [a temporary camp] for the night at Appomattox. Soon after Lee's departure I telegraphed to Washington as follows: "General Lee surrendered the Army of Northern Virginia this afternoon on terms proposed by myself. The accompanying additional correspondence will show the conditions fully. . . ."

> When news of the surrender first reached our lines our men commenced [began] firing a salute of a hundred guns in honor of the victory. I at once sent word, however, to have it stopped. The Confederates were now our prisoners, and we did not want to exult [celebrate or rejoice] over their downfall.

Union general Ulysses S. Grant. *From the Brady National Photographic Art Gallery. Courtesy of the Library of Congress.*

were and always would be fellow citizens, and the moment the fighting stopped he believed that they ought to begin behaving that way." The remaining Confederate armies all surrendered over the next few weeks. The soldiers returned home to begin the long process of rebuilding their lives.

Wilmer McLean was reluctant to allow the two generals to meet in his home. He knew that violence had followed the first time he helped the army, and he was determined to protect

Soldiers stand outside of Wilmer McLean's house in Appomattox Court House, Virginia, during Confederate general Robert E. Lee's surrender to Union general Ulysses S. Grant. *Photograph by Timothy O'Sullivan. Courtesy of the Library of Congress.*

Cover of *In My Father's House*. *Reproduced by permission of Scholastic, Inc.*

his family from the effects of the war. No one knows why McLean changed his mind and provided his parlor as the site of the historic meeting. But his home did suffer some damage as a result. As Rinaldi mentions in *In My Father's House,* Union officers took most of the contents of the parlor for souvenirs. They stole his marble tables and candlesticks, cut pieces of fabric from his sofa, and even took his young daughter's rag doll.

"These armies tore my place on Bull Run all to pieces, and kept running over it backward and forward till no man could live there, so I just sold out and came here, two hundred miles away, hoping I should never see a soldier again," McLean told General Edward Porter Alexander (1835–1910), as Alexander reported in his memoirs, *Military Memoirs of a Confederate.* "And now, just look around you! Not a fence-rail is left on the place, the last guns trampled down all my crops, and Lee surrenders to Grant in my house."

McLean's Confederate money became worthless after the war ended. He sold the historic house in Appomattox and returned to the Manassas area with his family. He served in various government jobs during the 1870s. Wilmer McLean died in June 1882. It was only after his death that the story of his unusual role in the Civil War became known.

Plot and characters of *In My Father's House*

In My Father's House begins in 1852, when Osceola ("Oscie") Mason is seven years old. She lives on a plantation called Yorkshire along the Bull Run River in Virginia. Her family owns fourteen slaves who act as servants in their home and work in their fields. Oscie's beloved father died several years ago. She is upset that her mother, Virginia Mason, is about to marry Will McLean. McLean is a merchant who used to do business with her father. Oscie opposes the marriage because she does not like McLean. She has also heard gossip about McLean and worries that he is only marrying Virginia for her money.

Since her father died, strong-willed Oscie has thought of herself as the head of the household, which also includes her older sister, Maria, and her younger sister, Sarah. Will McLean admires Oscie's spirit, but he also thinks she is too wild and needs discipline. McLean hires a tutor for Oscie and her sisters. Elvira Buttonworth, called Button for short, is from the North. She opposes slavery. In fact, her father helps slaves escape from the South and reach freedom in the North through a network of safe houses known as the Underground Railroad. Button teaches Oscie about math, literature, and music. She also teaches her manners, including when to speak her mind and when to keep quiet. Most importantly, Button teaches Oscie about the political situation in the United States at that time. She helps Oscie understand the issues that are dividing the country and leading toward the Civil War.

Will McLean also buys a slave named Mary Ann from a nearby plantation. Mary Ann has been dating Allie, one of the slaves at Yorkshire. McLean buys her so that they can be together. He also wants Mary Ann to care for the children he and Virginia plan to have. But Oscie has heard nasty rumors about Mary Ann and thinks she is a witch. She is also surprised that McLean has agreed to buy a slave, since he has made it clear that he does not like slavery. "I'm not an abolitionist, Oscie," McLean tells her. "But I am a realist. I was cared for by nigra [Negro] servants as a child. And I love the South. But I hate the slave system. And as a merchant, I know our cotton makes a long journey to the North to be manufactured into goods that come back to us at terrible prices."

In the spring of 1853, Oscie's mother announces that she is pregnant. Oscie wants to make sure that Mary Ann is not allowed to care for the new baby. She tries to convince her mother that Mary Ann is a witch. She also tries to talk Will McLean into putting Mary Ann to work in the fields, far away from the children. When they do not listen to her warnings, Oscie decides to show them that Mary Ann is crazy. One day, Oscie steals the shawl that Mary Ann always wears over her shoulders. Just as she expected, Mary Ann has a fit. But Will McLean convinces Mary Ann to show Oscie why she always wears the shawl. It turns out that she has terrible scars on her back from being whipped by her former owner. Oscie is shocked to learn that some people treat their slaves so cruelly. She still does not trust Mary Ann, but she begins to feel some sympathy toward her.

Tragedy strikes the family in the winter of 1854. Little Sarah slips out of the house unnoticed and goes ice skating on the creek by herself. She falls through the ice and dies a few days later. In their grief, the family blames Mary Ann for not watching Sarah more closely. Will McLean wants to sell Mary Ann, but Oscie and her mother talk him out of it. Still, McLean punishes Mary Ann by making her work in the fields. A short time later, Oscie finds out that Mary Ann is pregnant, but she does not tell her stepfather. She later regrets this decision. When Mary Ann suffers a miscarriage—possibly from working too hard in the fields—Oscie feels that she is to blame for not speaking up.

The story moves forward to 1860. The bitter disagreements between the North and the South over slavery and other issues are quickly leading toward war. Oscie and her family watch the political situation in the North very carefully. When the Southern states leave the Union and form the Confederacy, life becomes dangerous for Button as a Northerner in the South. She leaves the family and goes to Washington, D.C., where she serves as a nurse for wounded soldiers during the war.

Oscie is sixteen years old when the Civil War begins in 1861. In June of that year, a group of Confederate officers shows up at Yorkshire, including General Pierre G. T. Beauregard and Captain Edward Porter Alexander. Oscie shows Alexander, known as Alex, around the countryside and ends up falling in love with him, even though he is married.

Will McLean worries about the approaching war. He knows that the South is going to suffer, and he is determined to protect and provide for his family. As the Confederate forces prepare for battle, McLean decides to move his family away from the plantation. Shortly before they leave, Oscie has a confrontation with Mary Ann in the herb garden. A spiteful Mary Ann informs Oscie that she plans to tell her stepfather that she has been riding all around with Alex. Once Will McLean realizes that people are talking about Oscie's relationship with the married soldier, he makes them stop seeing each other.

McLean takes his family to live with relatives in Charlottesville, Virginia. The house at Yorkshire becomes Beauregard's headquarters, and the barn is turned into a hospital for treating wounded soldiers. In July 1861, the land around the plantation is the site of the first major battle of the Civil War. One of Oscie's neighbors, an elderly woman named Mrs. Henry, refuses to leave her home as the war approaches. Some of the most intense fighting in the First Battle of Bull Run takes place at Henry House Hill. The house is destroyed, and Mrs. Henry is killed.

As the war drags on, McLean becomes a "speculator." He uses his talents and contacts as a merchant to buy supplies and then sell them again at a high price. The South experiences severe shortages of goods during the war, so McLean is able to make a lot of money. But most Southerners look down upon speculators who make a profit on the war. They feel that these men are partly responsible for the shortages and the high prices of goods. Will McLean knows that some people do not approve of his actions. He feels guilty, but he claims that he must do whatever is necessary to support his family.

Oscie understands that the war put her stepfather in a difficult position. "I felt something stirring in me, some sadness and sympathy and affection for this man," she says. "The candle was going out in the South and he knew how hopeless it all was. And he'd made a clearing for himself in the midst of all the pageantry and horror of the war, like some bantam rooster in the barnyard, determined to do anything to take care of those who belonged to him. I respected him more that night than I had in a long time. And I think he felt about me in kind."

In 1863, Oscie and her family move to the quiet town of Appomattox Court House in the southern part of Virginia. When she arrives at her new home, Oscie is surprised to find Mary Ann there because Will McLean recently freed all of the family's slaves. Several loyal house servants decided to remain with the family, though, and when Mary Ann's husband left to help the Union army, McLean agreed to take Mary Ann with them to Appomattox. After they arrive, Mary Ann makes friends with the free black people who live in the town. She brags that Will McLean regularly sends his family coffee, sugar, cloth, and other goods that are in short supply.

One day, Oscie and Maria go to the general store to buy some dress patterns. The store owner and several angry customers confront the girls about their stepfather's activities as a speculator. But a local boy named Thomas Tibbs steps in to defend them. Tom tells Oscie that he is planning to join a famous Confederate cavalry group led by John Singleton Mosby (1833–1916), known as Mosby's Rangers. "I'm out for the adventure of it, before [the war] ends. That's why I'm joining Mosby," he explains. "As for the South . . . our way of life is fast disappearing, Oscie. I can't bother my head wondering if it's right or not. It's all I've ever known, and I'll defend it long as I can." Before Tom leaves, he and Oscie become close friends and fall in love. Oscie wants to become engaged to Tom, but Will McLean refuses to give his permission until the war is over.

One day, Oscie must go to the train station to pick up some supplies sent by Will McLean. Mary Ann tries to warn her that she should take someone with her, but Oscie does not listen. As it turns out, there is an angry mob of people at the train station. They are waiting for Oscie to claim the supplies so they can steal them from her. The scene turns ugly, but then Tom and the free blacks from town come to the rescue. Grateful for their help, Oscie shares the supplies with them. She then learns that her rescuers had been sent to the station by Mary Ann, who was worried about Oscie's safety. When she goes home, she and Mary Ann agree to put their differences aside and trust one another.

The story moves forward to 1865, when Oscie is twenty years old. Despite McLean's efforts to protect his family, the war is quickly approaching their new home. Confederate general Robert E. Lee is forced to move his troops out of Richmond and across the Appomattox River. Oscie's mother wants to help feed the hungry Confederate troops as they pass through town. But Will McLean wants to lock the doors and hide his family. After several days of arguing, the women of the family finally convince him that they should help in whatever way they can. McLean talks to an officer friend of his and agrees to provide his home as the site of the historic meeting between Lee and Union general Ulysses S. Grant. Although the town is surrounded by armies, Oscie realizes that they are "waiting. Not to fight this time. But to move toward each other and come together finally, as one people. All kinds of people, but together as one country again. One country, with room for all kinds of people."

After Lee surrenders to Grant in McLean's parlor, Union soldiers strip the place of everything they can carry. Everyone wants a souvenir of the occasion, which marks the end of four long years of war. The following day, Oscie watches as the Confederate soldiers in Lee's army lay down their weapons. It is a solemn ceremony, and both sides salute each other.

Even though the war is over, Oscie realizes that many questions remain to be answered. For example, she wonders what effect the violence of the war will have on the men who fought in it, and what the former slaves will do with their freedom. As the novel ends, Oscie goes with the Tibbs family to pick up Tom, who has received a minor wound. She and Will McLean have a final talk, and she asks for his blessing. "I was asking him to let me go. The way a girl asks her father," Oscie realizes. "And he was getting ready to release me. The way a father does, when he knows a girl's grown."

Style and themes in *In My Father's House*

Rinaldi wrote *In My Father's House* in "first person," meaning that the narrator is also a character in the story. Many of Rinaldi's books feature a teenage girl as the main character. In this case, Oscie tells the story of how Will McLean married her mother and became the head of their family. The events in the novel take place over a period of thirteen years in Oscie's life. She is a child when the story begins, and she has grown into a young woman by the time it ends.

At several points in the book, Oscie makes it clear that she is looking back on events that occurred earlier. In the first chapter, for example, she says: "When I was growing up at Yorkshire . . . nobody ever dreamed the North and the South would pick our front lawn to start their old war on. Although I suppose armies have to commence killing each other someplace. . . . But for me the confusion and mayhem came before that, when Will McLean came into our lives. Which should tell a person how I felt about him when he first came to us."

One of the main themes of *In My Father's House* is the developing relationship between Oscie and her stepfather. At first, even though she is only seven years old, Oscie views herself as the head of the family and resents Will McLean for intruding into her life. She often challenges his authority and spitefully passes on her dislike of him to the servants. When Button comes to tutor the Mason girls, the main thing Oscie hopes to learn is a way to "best" (get the best of) Will McLean.

Over time, however, Oscie begins to see evidence of McLean's deep devotion to her family. First, she is struck by his genuine feelings of grief when her sister Sarah dies. Then she recognizes how wise and open-minded he was to bring Button from the North to be their tutor as the two parts of the country prepared to go to war. She comes to respect his feelings about slavery and his beliefs about how the South must change in order to survive. During the war, Oscie is impressed by McLean's willingness to do whatever is necessary to protect and provide for his family. As an adult, Oscie recognizes the sacrifices her stepfather made for her and appreciates him for it. In the end, she realizes that Will McLean has been a good father to her.

Another theme in the novel centers around the way that war changes people. Oscie grows up during the Civil War. She is forced to leave her childhood home and begin a new life in an unfamiliar town. She worries about Tom, Alex, and other people she knows who are involved in the fighting. She also must take care of her family while Will McLean is away. By the time the Civil War ends, Oscie realizes that she is a different person. "Manassas was another world, another time," she says. "We're none of us the same. We all left part of ourselves back there."

Will McLean also changed because of his wartime experiences. He always struggled with the idea of owning slaves and disliked the way things were done in the Old South. He considered himself a representative of the future, or the New South. When the war began, McLean was determined to do whatever was necessary to protect his family. He became a speculator and made a profit by trading goods that were in short supply. Ashamed of his actions, he tells Oscie that the war brought out his true nature: "I never was the man your mother thought I was back at Manassas before the war. . . . I was never comfortable in the role of slave owner. You knew me for what I was. And I told you in the beginning that change was coming. . . . The war brought out the real Will McLean, Oscie. And he stands before you now." Oscie refuses to accept McLean's statement. She tells him that he just needs to find a way to restore his family's faith in him. This is why McLean agrees to allow the generals to meet in his house to negotiate an end to the Civil War.

Research and Activity Ideas

1) Throughout *In My Father's House,* there is a great deal of tension between Oscie Mason and Will McLean. How does Oscie's relationship with her stepfather change over time? Find specific incidents in the novel that change the way she feels about him.

2) At one point early in the novel, Oscie says, "I didn't realize how little I knew until . . . Mary Ann came to live with us." What did Oscie learn from Mary Ann?

3) Ann Rinaldi based *In My Father's House* on the true story of Wilmer McLean and his family. She did research to find the basic facts about people who really existed, and then used her imagination to fill in the gaps and create an interesting story. Conduct research on a not-so-famous person from the Civil War era. Select an incident from his or her life and use your imagination and what you know about the war to turn it into a short story.

Related Titles

Fleischman, Paul. *Bull Run.* New York: HarperCollins Publishers, 1993. *A novel in which sixteen different characters tell about their experiences during the first major battle of the Civil War.*

Marrin, Albert. *Unconditional Surrender: U. S. Grant and the Civil War* and *Virginia's General: Robert E. Lee and the Civil War.* New York: Atheneum, 1994. *Juvenile biographies of the two great generals who met to negotiate terms of surrender to end the Civil War.*

Mitchell, Margaret. *Gone with the Wind.* New York: Macmillan, 1936. *An epic novel about the life of a wealthy young Southern woman during and after the Civil War.*

Rinaldi, Ann. *The Last Silk Dress.* New York: Holiday House, 1988. *A novel about a young girl who helps the Confederate Army during the Civil War.*

Where to Learn More About . . .

Ann Rinaldi and *In My Father's House*

Authors and Artists for Young Adults. Vol. 15. Detroit: Gale, 1995.

Contemporary Authors Online. Detroit: Gale, 2001.

Dessau, D. Ilana, and Jenna Galley. "Learning about Ann Rinaldi." *Kay E. Vandergrift's Special Interest Page.* [Online] http://www.scils.rutgers.edu/special/kay/rinaldi.html (accessed on August 17, 2001).

Reichard, Sue. "Eve Bunting and Ann Rinaldi." *Suite101.com* [Online] http://www.suite101.com/article.cfm/525/6008 (last accessed on August 17, 2001).

St. James Guide to Young Adult Writers. 2d ed. Detroit: St. James Press, 1999.

Something about the Author. Vol. 51. Detroit: Gale, 1988.

Stanek, L.W. *Teaching Guide to* Wolf by the Ears *and* In My Father's House *by Ann Rinaldi* (pamphlet). New York: Scholastic, 1995.

Wilmer McLean and the Confederate Surrender at Appomattox

Appomattox Court House National Historic Park. *McLean House.* [Online] http://www.nps.gov/apco/mchs.htm (accessed on August 17, 2001).

Archer, Jules. *A House Divided: The Lives of Ulysses S. Grant and Robert E. Lee.* New York: Scholastic, 1995.

Catton, Bruce. *The Civil War.* New York: American Heritage Press, 1971, 1985.

Cauble, Frank P. *Biography of Wilmer McLean, May 3, 1814–June 3, 1882.* Lynchburg, VA: H. E. Howard, 1987.

Cauble, Frank P. *Surrender Proceedings, Appomattox Court House, April 9, 1865.* Lynchburg, VA: H. E. Howard, 1987.

Davis, Burke. *The Civil War: Strange and Fascinating Facts.* Wing Books, 1994.

Dowdey, Clifford. *Lee's Last Campaign: The Story of Lee and His Men against Grant.* Boston: Little, Brown, 1960. Reprint, Lincoln: University of Nebraska Press, 1993.

Grant, Ulysses S. *The Personal Memoirs of U. S. Grant.* 1885. Reprint, New York: Da Capo Press, 1982.

The Red Badge of Courage

Written by Stephen Crane

The Red Badge of Courage ranks as one of the most famous novels in American literature. This 1895 work was written by a young novelist and journalist named Stephen Crane (1871–1900). It describes the experiences and emotions of one Union soldier who takes part in an unnamed but bloody battle of the American Civil War (1861–65). Crane's book was one of the first works of fiction to explore realistically emotions such as courage and fear on the battlefield. In fact, his descriptions of the chaos and horror of combat were so powerful and authentic that many readers mistakenly believed that Crane had served as a soldier in the conflict. Today, *The Red Badge of Courage* is widely regarded as the finest novel ever written about the American Civil War.

Biography of author Stephen Crane

Stephen Townley Crane was born on November 1, 1871, in Newark, New Jersey. He was the youngest of fourteen children born to Jonathan Townley, a Methodist minister, and Mary Helen (Peck) Crane. After his father's death in 1880, young Crane came under the influence of his worldly older brothers.

Stephen Crane, author of
The Red Badge of Courage.
Reproduced by permission
of the Corbis Corporation.

By his mid-teens, Crane had turned into a rebellious youth who rejected his parents' religious teachings. He also developed a strong interest in writing and journalism during this period.

In 1888, Crane enrolled at Hudson River Institute and Claverack College, where he became better known for his performance on the baseball field than in the classroom. After graduation, he briefly attended Lafayette College in Pennsylvania and Syracuse University in New York. But his studies bored him, and in 1891 he moved to New York City to work as a reporter.

During the next few years, Crane struggled to support himself as a journalist, a poet, and a fiction writer. He spent much of this time exploring and writing about New York's most poverty-stricken streets and neighborhoods, where thousands of families waged a daily struggle just to survive. In 1893, he published his first novel, *Maggie: A Girl of the Streets.* This work highlighted the terrible social conditions that Crane had witnessed in the Bowery and other poor areas of New York. The book established Crane as a bright new writing talent.

Crane then turned his attention to the American Civil War. This conflict had ended in 1865, six years before his birth. But Crane had grown up in a society in which memories of the war were still very fresh and painful. As a youngster, he had heard many stories about the war from veterans—including his eldest brother. In addition, he had read many memoirs that had been published by men who had fought for the North or the South.

But Crane felt that all of the Civil War stories he heard and read were incomplete. In his view, the stories told what the participants had done in the war but did not explain how they had felt as they went into battle or buried their fellow soldiers. Crane decided that he wanted to write a novel that would show what it must have felt like to have been a soldier in that brutal war.

The Red Badge of Courage: An Episode of the American Civil War first appeared in abbreviated form in a newspaper called the *Philadelphia Press* from December 3 to December 8, 1894. A shortened version of the story then appeared in dozens of newspapers across the country over the next several months. But Crane wanted to publish his novel in its complete form. As a result, he devoted a great deal of time to finding a publisher. Finally, D. Appleton and Company published Crane's novel in October 1895.

The publication of *The Red Badge of Courage* changed Crane's life. Its status as a bestseller enabled the author to rise out of poverty for the first time in years. In addition, the novel made Crane famous. Reviewers were so impressed with the book's unforgettable imagery (the use of figurative language or vivid descriptions) and intensity that they began describing the author as America's next great writer. In fact, Crane's writing was so convincing that many readers assumed that he had actually fought in the Civil War. Some veterans of the war even publicly claimed that they had served with Crane.

In the months following the publication of *The Red Badge of Courage,* Crane completed a wide variety of writing projects. These works included a poetry collection (*The Black Riders, and Other Lines*); assignments to write newspaper articles, with one assignment involving Crane in a tragic shipwreck (see box) while he was covering the Cuban revolt against Spain; and several acclaimed Civil War stories. After a while, however, he stopped writing fiction about the Civil War because he feared that readers were beginning to think of him only as a war writer. He even expressed bitterness about his decision to write *The Red Badge of Courage* in the first place.

In 1897, Crane moved to England with Cora Taylor, with whom he had a common-law marriage (a marriage that exists by mutual agreement without a civil or religious ceremony). Over the next few years, Crane worked as a journalist for a variety of American and foreign newspapers. During this time, he reported on both the Greco-Turkish War (1897) and the Spanish-American War (1898). His experiences covering these wars reassured him that *The Red Badge of Courage* had accurately captured the chaos and terror of warfare. In 1900, Crane's health deteriorated sharply.

Stephen Crane's Courage at Sea

In late 1896, Stephen Crane received a newspaper assignment to go to Cuba, a small country located south of Florida in the Caribbean Sea. The assignment called for him to cover a Cuban revolt against Spain, which had long exercised control over the small island nation. On December 31, 1896, Crane set sail from the United States to Cuba on a ship called the *Commodore*. The crew of this ship consisted of Cuban rebels who had loaded the *Commodore* with weapons to use against the Spanish-led government forces.

During the ship's first night at sea, however, it ran into a terrible storm. Crane helped the captain and crew throughout the night as they tried to keep the boat afloat. Finally, however, the crew abandoned ship and piled into lifeboats. Crane and the Cubans fought off sharks and high waves throughout the remainder of the night.

When newspaper reporters learned about the sinking of the *Commodore* from other ships, the accident became front-page news. In fact, some reporters stated that Crane had drowned in the tragedy. But Crane did not perish in the shipwreck. A dozen men lost their lives in the tragedy, but seventeen men—including Crane—survived. They rode out the storm and managed to reach the safety of the Florida coastline the next day.

According to the sailors of the *Commodore*, Crane acted calmly throughout the frightening night at sea. "That newspaper man was a nervy [brave] man," said one crew member. "He didn't seem to know what fear was. . . . He never quailed [showed fear] when he saw the raging waves and knew the vessel was sinking, and that it was only a matter of time when we would be at the mercy of the sea in a small dinghy [boat]." The captain of the boat also praised the writer for his bravery at sea. In fact, Crane was credited with saving one Cuban sailor from drowning during the ordeal.

A few months later, Crane wrote a short story, "The Open Boat," based upon his shipwreck experience. Today, it is regarded as one of the author's finest short stories.

He died of tuberculosis, a disease that attacks the lungs and other vital organs, on June 5, 1900, in Badenweiler, Germany.

Historical background of *The Red Badge of Courage*

The Red Badge of Courage takes place during the American Civil War. This conflict began in 1861. It pitted the nation's

Northern and Southern states against one another in an epic military struggle. The war came about when the Southern states tried to leave the United States and form their own nation, called the Confederate States of America, or the Confederacy. The South's desire to secede (withdraw) from the United States stemmed from years of disagreement with the Northern states over slavery, the limits of federal power, and other issues. But the North—or the Union as it was known during the war—refused to let the South break up the country without a fight. As a result, the divided nation endured four years of terrible bloodshed. When the North finally won the war in 1865, approximately four million Southern African Americans were released from slavery. But the Civil War took a fearsome toll on both sides. Approximately six hundred thousand soldiers lost their lives in the conflict. In addition, property damage from the war reached an estimated $5 billion, with most of the damage occurring in the South.

Crane never identifies the battle that he describes in *The Red Badge of Courage*. But historians agree that the clash in which

Dead soldiers lie behind a stone wall in Fredericksburg, Virginia, following the Battle of Chancellorsville.
Photograph by Andrew J. Russell. Courtesy of the National Archives and Records Administration.

Union general Joseph Hooker, whose Army of the Potomac was defeated by Confederate general Robert E. Lee's Army of Northern Virginia in the Battle of Chancellorsville. *Courtesy of the National Archives and Records Administration.*

main character Henry Fleming fights is the Battle of Chancellorsville. This battle took place near Chancellorsville, a small village located between the towns of Orange and Fredericksburg, Virginia. It raged from May 1 to May 4, 1863, and proved to be one of the most important battles of the entire war.

The Battle of Chancellorsville came about when Union general Joseph Hooker (1814–1879) led his 130,000-man Army of the Potomac into Virginia. Hooker hoped to find and destroy the Army of Northern Virginia, which was the Confederacy's largest force. Once the Army of Northern Virginia was defeated, Union strategists knew that their troops would be able to capture Richmond, the capital of the Confederacy. They believed that if Richmond was captured, the entire Confederacy would collapse.

But as Hooker's army crossed the Rappahannock River and marched toward Chancellorsville, Confederate general Robert E. Lee (1807–1870) launched a plan to defeat the enemy. Lee knew that his sixty-thousand-man Army of Northern Virginia was badly outnumbered by Hooker's massive force. But the Confederate general believed that he could use surprise attacks and strategic troop movements to confuse the Union army. Lee's plan worked. After four days of terrible fighting, Hooker withdrew his army back into Northern territory. Union forces suffered an estimated seventeen thousand casualties (dead, wounded, and missing soldiers) during this time. Southern casualties, meanwhile, numbered about thirteen thousand.

The Confederate victory at Chancellorsville ruined the Union's plans to attack Richmond. It also enabled Lee to launch an invasion of the North in June 1863. Lee's forces marched through Northern territory for a month. Their presence deeply alarmed the Northern people, who began to wonder if the Union might lose the war despite its advantages in troops and weaponry. But in July 1863, Lee's Army of Northern Virginia suffered a decisive defeat at Gettysburg, Pennsylvania. The South never fully recovered from this loss. The defeat forced Lee's battered Army of Northern Virginia to retreat back into Southern territory. In addition, it gave Union soldiers renewed confidence that they would eventually win the war.

Scholars believe that *The Red Badge of Courage* takes place during the Battle of Chancellorsville for several reasons. Crane refers in his novel to geographical landmarks like the Rappahannock River, which flowed past Chancellorsville. In addition, the woods and hills that are described in Crane's book match the terrain upon which the Battle of Chancellorsville was fought. Even the weather described in *The Red Badge of Courage* matches the weather that passed through Chancellorsville in early May 1863.

Most importantly, the bloody clash that is described in *The Red Badge of Courage* closely parallels many aspects of the actual Battle of Chancellorsville. For example, Crane describes the military leaders of the Northern army as incompetent officers who fail to provide good leadership. Many historians have described the Union officers at Chancellorsville in the same way. In addition, the Union army suffers from widespread desertions (leaving military service without permission with no intention of returning) both before and during the battle in Crane's novel. This reflects events at Chancellorsville, where many Union soldiers fled the field of battle. In fact, one Union officer, Washington Roebling (1837–1926), recalled in *Battles and Leaders of the Civil War* that the Union army at Chancellorsville behaved "for all the world like a stampede of cattle. . . . A multitude [great number] of yelling, struggling men who had thrown away their muskets [rifles], panting for breath, their faces distorted by fear, filled the road as far as the eye could reach." In addition, the overall flow of the Battle of Chancellorsville, which featured many surprise attacks and counterattacks, can be seen in the narrative of Crane's novel.

Finally, scholars note that the character of Henry Fleming (see box) later appears in one of Stephen Crane's short stories. In this story, titled "The Veteran," the character of Fleming admits that he ran away in fear during the Battle of Chancellorsville.

Henry Fleming's Final Act of Bravery

Henry Fleming, the main character in *The Red Badge of Courage,* later died in a short story that was written by Stephen Crane several months after the publication of his famous novel. In this short story, called "The Veteran," Henry Fleming is no longer a young soldier. In fact, he has grown into an old man. He leads a quiet existence among townspeople who regard him as a genuine Civil War hero.

Fleming's grandson, Jimmy, also sees him as a hero. But when Fleming is asked if he was ever afraid in battle, he honestly admits that he ran away from the enemy during the early stages of the Battle of Chancellorsville. This admission shocks young Jimmy, who feels deep disappoint-ment and humiliation. At the end of the story, though, Fleming shows great courage. He bravely enters a barn that has erupted in flames in order to rescue horses that are trapped in the building. The roof of the barn collapses before Fleming can escape the blaze, killing the old Civil War soldier. But Crane's description of his death suggests that Fleming's brave spirit lives on: "When the roof fell in, a great funnel of smoke swarmed toward the sky, as if the old man's mighty spirit, released from its body—a little bottle—had swelled like the genie of fable. The smoke was tinted rose-hue from the flames, and perhaps the unut-terable [impossible to describe] midnights of the universe will have no power to daunt [frighten] the color of this soul."

Plot and characters of *The Red Badge of Courage*

The Red Badge of Courage takes place during the Ameri-can Civil War, which lasted from 1861 to 1865. The central character in the novel is Henry Fleming, a young man from a small town in Ohio. A Northerner, he has voluntarily joined the Union army out of feelings of patriotism and a fierce desire to prove his manhood on the field of battle. As the novel begins, however, Fleming wonders if his visions of military heroism will ever come true. He spends day after day in an army camp, where he and his fellow soldiers have settled into a boring routine of marching, drilling, and camp chores. But when rumors of an approaching clash with the enemy circu-late through the camp, Fleming begins to fear that he will not perform bravely in the upcoming battle.

Fleming's regiment is then ordered to break camp and strike out in the direction of the enemy. As the Union troops travel across the countryside, Fleming's anxieties grow. Concerned that he might not be as brave as the rest of the soldiers around him, he talks to a soldier named Wilson in hopes of receiving reassurance. But Wilson is convinced that he is going to die in the upcoming battle. In fact, he gives Fleming several letters intended for his loved ones and asks him to keep them for him.

During several long days of marching, Fleming's Union regiment sees frightening signs of war, including dead bodies and fleeing soldiers. Finally, Fleming and his fellow soldiers confront Confederate forces in battle. When Fleming first comes under fire from the enemy, he stands firm and shoots back. His performance in this first skirmish (small battle) reassures him of his bravery. But a second wave of attackers then rushes forward, and the battle dissolves into chaos. Overwhelmed with fear, Fleming and many of his fellow soldiers flee into the woods. As he runs away, Fleming makes a variety of excuses for his behavior. Young Fleming's desperate flight through the tangled forest continues until he stumbles across the corpse of a soldier in a "chapel," an opening in the woods.

After encountering the corpse in the woods, Fleming meets other wounded and dying Union soldiers. His exposure to their injuries makes him wish that he had his own "red badge of courage" (wound) as proof that he had fought well. As he continues his wanderings, he recognizes one of the injured soldiers as Jim Conklin, a childhood friend. Fleming and a wounded soldier known as the tattered man watch over Conklin during his last moments of life. After Conklin dies, Fleming leaves the

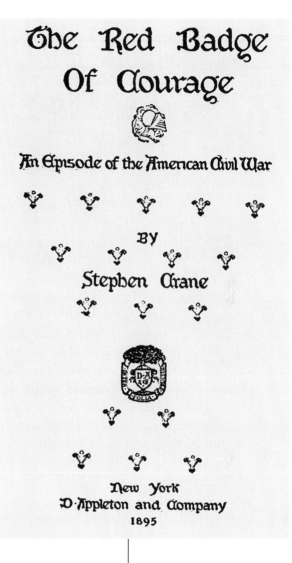

The Red Badge Of Courage

An Episode of the American Civil War

BY

Stephen Crane

New York
D. Appleton and Company
1895

Cover of an early edition of *The Red Badge of Courage*. *Public domain.*

dying tattered man behind and continues his flight. As he moves through the woods, he is consumed with guilt over his desertion of the tattered soldier, who had treated him kindly.

As Fleming resumes his wandering, he considers returning to his military unit. But he hesitates because he is afraid that he might be recognized as a deserter or fail again on the field of battle. He then encounters another group of retreating Union soldiers. One of these soldiers angrily clubs Fleming in the head with his rifle. The blow draws blood, and Fleming is forced to wear a bandage to stop the bleeding. He then finds his way back to his unit with the help of an unknown soldier. Upon his return, he explains the blood-stained bandage around his head by claiming that he was shot in battle. This story impresses the soldiers, who call him a hero. The symbolism of the bloody bandage—a fake red badge of courage—also makes Fleming think of himself as a brave and noble soldier, even though he knows that he did not receive the wound in battle.

Fleming is then reunited with Wilson, who survived the battle. The battered regiment then triumphs in another brief clash with the enemy. Fleming performs well in the skirmish, but when he and Wilson attempt to retrieve water for the regiment, he hears Union officers talk about the soldiers in dismissive tones. He realizes that the officers regard his life and those of the other soldiers as unimportant.

This knowledge enrages Fleming, who then leads his regiment in yet another battle against Confederate troops. In this clash, he saves the American flag from being captured and leads his fellow soldiers to victory. His performance is recognized by the regiment's officers, who praise both him and Wilson for their fighting spirit. Fleming then spends the last pages of the novel recalling his battlefield experiences and feelings of the past few days. As he prepares for another battle, he decides that he has finally achieved a "quiet manhood . . . of sturdy and strong blood."

Style and themes in *The Red Badge of Courage*

Writing realistically about war and people. Stephen Crane's *The Red Badge of Courage* was one of the first American novels that described war in a realistic way. Before Crane's book, most stories about the Civil War or other armed conflicts portrayed war as a glorious, patriotic way for young men to prove their manhood. These works did not talk about the terror that soldiers felt before going into battle. They also did not dwell on the awful wounds that crippled or killed hundreds of thousands of young men. Crane, however, showed that war was frightening and brutal. In fact, some people regard *The Red Badge of Courage* as America's first major antiwar novel.

Crane's novel was unusual for its time in other ways as well. Unlike most other writers of his era, Crane used the language and speaking styles of ordinary people in his book. In addition, he focused on the emotions and experiences of ordinary soldiers at a time when most other books about war focused on generals and other military leaders. Finally, Crane wrote *The Red Badge of Courage* at a time when most American literature featured romantic plots and polite, innocent characters. This light subject matter did not offend readers, but it also did not require readers to think very much about important issues. Crane's novel, on the other hand, challenged readers to examine their beliefs about the true nature of warfare.

Crane also used Henry Fleming's feelings of cowardice and bravery to explore American ideas about manhood and maturity. Some readers believe that *The Red Badge of Courage* is a story that shows how Fleming's frightening wartime experiences transform him from an innocent, sheltered boy into a brave, mature man. But other readers claim that Crane ends the novel in a way that suggests that Fleming has not yet achieved true manhood.

Naturalism and impressionism. Crane's novel is told in the "third person." This term means that the narrator (teller of the story) is an outside observer (rather than a character) who describes the experiences and emotions of the book's characters for the reader. As *The Red Badge of Courage* progresses, this narrative point of view shifts back and forth from "naturalism" to "impressionism."

Naturalism is a kind of writing in which the author tries to show life as it truly is, including its most unattractive and frightening aspects. In fact, naturalism is based on the idea that the natural world is an unforgiving place that does not

Scene from the Battle of Chancellorsville.
Lithograph by Currier and Ives. Reproduced by permission of the Corbis Corporation.

care about the hopes or dreams of people. Naturalist literature also usually suggests that people have little or no control over their future. Instead, naturalism is based on the idea that one's experiences and behavior are controlled by one's emotions and surrounding social and economic conditions. Examples of naturalism in Crane's *The Red Badge of Courage* include graphic descriptions of warfare, realistic portraits of the soldiers' terror and confusion, and suggestions that nature is indifferent to human pain and suffering.

Impressionism, on the other hand, is a writing style that emphasizes the feelings and emotions of its characters. When Crane turns to this point of view, he does not try to provide readers with a realistic account of events. Instead, he concentrates on showing readers how Henry Fleming feels emotionally about his battlefield experiences. Fleming's thoughts and emotions may not be factually accurate, but they are still important because they show how his experiences shape his development as a person. Examples of impressionism in *The*

Experiencing the American Civil War

Media Adaptations of *The Red Badge of Courage*

Films:

In 1951, famous director John Huston (1906–1987) released a film version of *The Red Badge of Courage.* Huston once called it his best movie, but it failed to attract large audiences when it was released. World War II hero Audie Murphy (1924–1971) played the character of Henry Fleming in the film. Originally released by Universal Pictures, the film is currently available on video from MCA/Universal Home Video.

Audiotapes:

An abridged recording of the book, narrated by actor Richard Crenna (1927–), was produced in 1985 by Listen for Pleasure. It is available in two audiocassettes totaling 120 minutes. In addition, a complete audiotape of the book (three cassettes, 270 minutes), narrated by Frank Muller, was produced by Recorded Books in 1981.

A scene from the movie *The Red Badge of Courage* (1951) shows two Civil War soldiers holding the American flag together above a fallen soldier. *Reproduced by permission of the Kobal Collection.*

Red Badge of Courage include Crane's frequent use of color and animal imagery to show Fleming's emotional state of mind.

Color and animal imagery. Crane employs a great deal of color imagery throughout his novel. For example, he often uses the color red—the color of blood—when he describes Fleming's impressions of the war. At one point, Fleming describes a battle as sounding like a "crimson roar." In another chapter, he refers to war as a "red animal." As the story progresses, Fleming expresses a strong desire to gain a "red badge of courage"—a wound—to prove his bravery on the field of battle.

Another color that frequently appears in Crane's novel is blue. The author uses this color to emphasize his belief that the natural world does not care about the violence and death swirling around the two armies. For example, Fleming notices with "a flash of astonishment" that the sky retains a pleasant blue color throughout the battle, as if nature has not even noticed the pain and suffering of the humans struggling below.

Crane also employs animal imagery throughout *The Red Badge of Courage.* At the beginning of the book, for example, Crane compares the campfires of the distant Confederate camp to the red eyes of a fearsome animal. He also compares Fleming and other soldiers to various wild animals throughout the novel. Most critics feel that Crane makes these comparisons in order to emphasize his belief that the soldiers are trapped like animals in a world that does not care about them.

Symbolism. Crane uses a literary device known as "symbolism" throughout *The Red Badge of Courage.* Symbolism is an author's use of an object or an event to represent an idea or a concept. The most obvious symbol in Crane's novel is the blood-soaked bandage that Fleming wears after he is hit on the head. This wound is seen by Fleming and his fellow soldiers as a "red badge" that symbolizes courage, bravery, and manhood.

Research and Activity Ideas

1) After reading *The Red Badge of Courage,* study the events that took place during the actual Battle of Chancellorsville. Can you find ways in which Crane's novel mirrors the events in the actual battle? Are there ways in which the Battle of Chancellorsville was different from the battle described in Crane's book?

2) As you read *The Red Badge of Courage,* look for instances in which Crane uses flowers, woods, or colors as symbols. What points do you think the author is trying to make when he uses these various symbols?

3) After you finish reading Crane's novel, do you believe that young Henry Fleming has reached his goal of achieving manhood? Or do you think that he still lacks maturity and insight about his true character?

Related Titles

Foote, Shelby. *Shiloh*. New York: Dial Press, 1952. Reprint, New York: Vintage Books, 1991. *This novel describes the Battle of Shiloh from the perspective of many different participants.*

Hudgins, Andrew. "At Chancellorsville." In *After the Lost War: A Narrative*. Boston: Houghton Mifflin, 1988. *In this poem about the horrors of war, a young Confederate soldier in a ragged uniform debates whether to strip the clothing off the body of a dead Union soldier following the Battle of Chancellorsville.*

Murphy, Jim. *The Journal of James Edmond Pease, a Civil War Union Soldier.* New York: Scholastic, 1998. *In this novel, a sixteen-year-old Union soldier keeps a journal about the hardships of war and his experiences in battle.*

Where to Learn More About . . .

Stephen Crane and *The Red Badge of Courage*

Bloom, Harold, ed. *Modern Critical Views: Stephen Crane*. New York: Chelsea House, 1987.

Cady, Edwin H. *Stephen Crane*. Boston: Twayne, 1980.

Davis, Linda H. *Badge of Courage: The Life of Stephen Crane*. Boston: Houghton Mifflin, 1998.

Johnson, Claudia Durst. *Understanding The Red Badge of Courage*. Westport, CT: Greenwood Press, 1998.

Stephen Crane Society. [Online] http://home.earthlink.net/~warburg/ (accessed on August 20, 2001).

Sufrin, Mark. *Stephen Crane*. New York: Macmillan Publishing, 1992.

Wertheim, Stanley. *A Stephen Crane Encyclopedia*. Westport, CT: Greenwood Press, 1997.

The Battle of Chancellorsville

Kent, Zachary. *The Battle of Chancellorsville*. Chicago: Children's Press, 1994.

National Park Service. "The Battle of Chancellorsville, 1863." *Fredericksburg and Spotsylvania National Military Park*. [Online] http://www. nps.gov/frsp/chist.htm (accessed on August 20, 2001).

The Experiences of Civil War Soldiers

McPherson, James M. *For Cause and Comrades: Why Men Fought in the Civil War*. New York: Oxford University Press, 1997.

Mitchell, Reid. *Civil War Soldiers: Their Expectations and Their Experiences.* New York: Oxford University Press, 1988.

Reef, Catherine. *Civil War Soldiers.* New York: Twenty-First Century Books, 1993.

Soldier's Heart

Written by Gary Paulsen

Soldier's Heart is a novel based on the actual Civil War experiences of Charley Goddard, a fifteen-year-old boy who fought for the Union army as a member of the First Minnesota Volunteers. The book was written by Gary Paulsen (1939–), one of America's most popular and respected authors of books for children and young adults. In Soldier's Heart, Paulsen shows the full horror of war by describing not only the blood and gore of combat but its emotional impact on young Charley. By the end of the novel, Charley is transformed from an eager and innocent recruit into a crippled veteran haunted by his memories of the battlefield.

Soldier's Heart contains many graphic scenes of warfare. It also features two scenes in which horses are killed in brutal fashion and contains references to suicide.

Biography of author Gary Paulsen

Gary Paulsen was born May 17, 1939, in Minneapolis, Minnesota. His parents were Oscar, an army officer, and Eunice Paulsen. Looking back on his childhood, Paulsen describes

Gary Paulsen, author of
Soldier's Heart. Reproduced by permission of Gary Paulsen.

much of it as a nightmare. He was painfully shy, poor at sports, and an average student. In addition, his family frequently moved because of his father's military career, so he always seemed to be the newest kid in his class. Moreover, his alcoholic parents quarreled so fiercely that young Paulsen spent months at a time living with relatives in northern Minnesota. "My childhood—I just wanted to get through it alive," he recalled in an online interview with Scholastic.com. "I hated every minute of it. My parents fought and drank all the time. I was the least popular kid in school. I never had a date or went to a party in school. . . . I just was unpopular and ugly and had the wrong kind of clothes."

Paulsen's unhappy youth was relieved only by his love for literature. Guided toward reading by a friendly librarian, he spent hour after hour reading westerns, science fiction tales, or classic literature. "It was as though I had been dying of thirst and the librarian had handed me a five-gallon bucket of water," he said in *Something about the Author*. "I drank and drank." During this same period, he began his lifelong love affair with the outdoors, spending his summers working on Minnesota farms and his winters tending traplines in snowy Minnesota forestland.

After graduating from high school, Paulsen attended Bemidji College in Minnesota from 1957 to 1959. He then served in the U.S. Army from 1959 to 1962, where he received training in engineering. After leaving the army, he found employment in California's aerospace industry. But in his mid-twenties, he suddenly walked away from his job to try his hand as a writer. At first, he spent his days working as a proof-reader for a California-based magazine and his evenings laboring on his own personal writing projects. But after a year or so, he decided to return to his native Minnesota and devote all his energy to writing.

When Paulsen returned to Minnesota in the mid-1960s, he rented a cabin in the northern part of the state. He enjoyed this solitary lifestyle and found that it made it easy for him to concentrate on his writing. Over the next several years, he published a wide variety of novels, short stories, and articles, including a number of works that were targeted at young readers. He also married an artist named Ruth Ellen Wright in 1971. But a bitter legal fight over *Winterkill*, one of Paulsen's first young adult novels, nearly drove him away from writing forever. This fight erupted in 1977, when the author was sued by someone who claimed that the book was actually based on his family. Paulsen denied the charge, and he eventually won the court battle over the book. But the legal proceedings cost him his life savings and temporarily poisoned his love for writing.

Paulsen once again withdrew to a remote cabin deep in the Minnesota woods, where he spent his time trapping and dogsledding. For the next two years, he stayed away from writing. But a solitary, week-long dogsledding adventure in northern Minnesota changed his outlook on life. As the trip progressed, he developed a deep affection for his dogs and felt the frustration of his court battle melt away. When he returned home from his journey, he told his wife that his days of hunting and trapping were over. He also told her that he wanted to give writing another try.

As the 1980s progressed, Paulsen's career as a writer blossomed. During this time, he concentrated increasingly on writing books for young adults. He used his lifetime of experiences in the outdoors to create wilderness settings for many of these stories. For example, in both 1983 and 1985, Paulsen entered the famous Iditarod (eye-DIH-tah-rod) dogsledding race in Alaska. His memories of those races became the basis for *Dogsong*, one of his many award-winning novels for young adults.

Since that time, Paulsen has written numerous popular works for young adults. The best known of these books are the four volumes of his so-called "Brian" series. The first of these novels was *Hatchet*, published in 1987. This Newbery award-winning book tells the story of Brian Robeson, a teenage boy who learns to survive alone in the Canadian wilderness after a plane crash. Brian's outdoor adventures in subsequent books in the series—*The River* (1991), *Brian's Winter* (1996), and *Brian's Return* (1999)—gradually transform him into a lover of wilderness who feels most at home when he is exploring remote rivers and forests.

Today, Paulsen continues to divide his time between writing and trips into the outdoor world he loves so much. When a heart attack forced him to give up dogsledding in the mid-1990s, he turned to sailing. In mid-2001, he even embarked on a solo voyage by sailboat from Hawaii to Australia. Meanwhile, his deep desire to encourage young people to care about the world around them keeps him writing nearly every day, even though he has already written more than 175 books for children and young adults. "I probably have a hundred more books in me," he told Scholastic.com. "I work 18 hours a day, ever since I quit running dogs. I used to run dogs 18 hours a day. Now I write 18 hours a day."

Historical background of *Soldier's Heart*

Paulsen's novel is based on the actual life of Charley Goddard (1846–1868), who joined the Union forces as a member of the First Minnesota Volunteers at the age of fifteen. The author admits that not every event in his book actually occurred to young Charley. For instance, Charley Goddard never fought in the First Battle of Bull Run because he was suffering from dysentery (DIH-sen-teh-ree), a painful infection of the digestive system, when the battle took place. "But in all respects everything in the book happened, either to Charley or to men around him," wrote Paulsen in an author's note published in *Soldier's Heart*. In most other respects, the novel accurately follows events in Charley's life, from his decision to lie about his age to enlist in the First Minnesota Volunteers to the wounds he suffered at the Battle of Gettysburg.

Paulsen's book also provides an accurate picture of Charley's life after the war. "He was hit severely [at Gettysburg]," wrote Paulsen in his author's note, "and though they patched him up as best they could and he managed to fight in later actions, his wounds did not heal properly, nor did his mental anguish. When the war was finished he went back and tried to hold jobs and couldn't, eventually running for county clerk on the basis of his war record. He was elected, but before he could serve, his wounds and the stress took him and he died in December 1868. He was just twenty-three years old."

While writing *Soldier's Heart*, Paulsen made a special effort to provide an accurate picture of other historical aspects of the American Civil War (1861–65) as well. For example, he discusses the excitement that many young men felt before going off to war and the widespread belief in the North that the Union forces would defeat the Confederate army within a matter of months. He also points out that many soldiers in the Union army were most angry at the Southern states because they wanted to leave the United States and form their own country, not because of slavery. The South's use of black people as slaves was not a major issue for many Northerners at the beginning of the conflict. The author also provides information on the sorts of food that Civil War soldiers ate, the types of clothing they wore, and the uncomfortable, unsanitary conditions in which they lived. Most importantly, however, Paulsen provides young people with an unflinching, truthful description of the terrors of war and the emotional scars that warfare leaves on many of its participants.

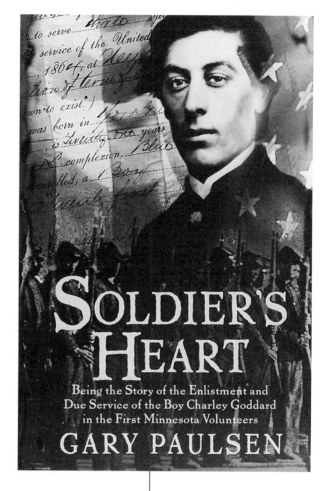

Cover of *Soldier's Heart*. Jacket illustration/montage © 1998 by Ericka Meltzer O'Rourke. Reproduced by permission of Dell Publishing Co. Photograph of Charles Goddard by Whitney; reproduced courtesy of the Minnesota Historical Society Collections.

Plot and characters of *Soldier's Heart*

In the opening pages of *Soldier's Heart,* readers are introduced to Charley Goddard, a fifteen-year-old Minnesota farmboy who decides to enlist in the Union army when war breaks out between America's Northern and Southern states. This conflict, known as the Civil War, or the War of the Rebellion, ultimately lasted for four years, from 1861 to 1865. More than six hundred thousand soldiers died in this war, which also freed four million African Americans from slavery. But when the war first flared up, Charley worried that if he did not enlist quickly, he would miss the entire conflict. "All the officers and politicians and newspapers said it would [last] a month or two, no longer," he noted.

A Confederate Soldier Remembers a Day of Death

On October 21, 1861, a seventeen-year-old Confederate soldier named Randolph Shotwell (1844–1885) took part in the Battle of Ball's Bluff, which ended in a victory for the South. This was not one of the major battles of the Civil War, but it still featured the major characteristics of larger battles like Gettysburg, Chancellorsville, and Antietam: death, pain, and terror. In the following excerpt from Shotwell's journal, first published in *The Papers of Randolph Abbott Shotwell* and later reprinted in Milton Meltzer's *Voices from the Civil War*, the young Southern private describes the last part of the battle, when the rebel army pushed their Northern enemies back to the brink of a high cliff overlooking a deep river:

Then ensued an awful spectacle! A kind of shiver ran through the huddled mass upon the brow [top] of the cliff; it gave way, rushed a few steps; then, in one wild, panic-stricken herd, rolled, leaped, tumbled over the precipice [cliff]! The descent is nearly perpendicular, with ragged, jutting crags, and a water-laved [water-washed] base. Screams of pain and terror filled the air. Men seemed suddenly bereft of [without] reason; they leaped over the bluff with muskets still in their clutch, threw themselves into the river without divesting themselves of their heavy accoutrements [gear], hence went to the bottom like lead. Others sprang down upon the heads and bayonets of those below. . . .

From the beginning of the battle a steady stream of wounded men had been trickling down the zigzag path leading to the narrow beach, whence the

Civil War soldiers find slain comrades on the bank of the Potomac River following the Battle of Ball's Bluff, Virginia. *Illustration by Alfred R. Waud. Originally published in* Harper's Weekly, *October 21, 1862. Courtesy of the Library of Congress.*

boats were to convey them to the island. As it happened, the two larger bateaux [flat-bottomed boats] were just starting with an overload when the torrent of terror-stricken fugitives rolled down the bluffs—upon them. Both boats were instantly submerged, and their cargoes of helpless human beings (crippled by wounds) were swept away to unknown graves! The whole surface of the river seemed filled with heads, struggling, screaming, fighting, dying! Man clutched at man, and the strong, who might have escaped, were dragged down by the weaker. Voices that strove to shout for help were stifled by the turbid [muddy], sullen waters of the swollen river and died away in gurgles. . . .

Eager to prove his bravery in battle, Charley bids good-bye to his mother and travels to a nearby fort, where he enlists in the First Minnesota Volunteers. He has to lie about his age to be accepted, for soldiers are supposed to be at least eighteen years old. But nobody questions his declaration that he is old enough to be a soldier, despite his youthful appearance. After a few weeks, Charley's company is ordered to report to Washington, D.C., where the main Union army is forming. As Charley and the other members of his company travel eastward by steamboat and train, townspeople along their route turn out to cheer them on. The celebrations, steamboat journeys, and train rides all delight Charley, who is still a simple farmboy at heart. "It was all new to him," wrote Paulsen. "Charley had never ridden on a steamboat, never marched in a parade or had pretty girls wave flags for him and hand him sweets."

In the next section of the book, however, Paulsen abruptly moves ahead in time and places Charley in the midst of his first battle against Confederate forces. This clash—the First Battle of Bull Run, in Virginia—is a terrifying experience for young Charley, who keeps thinking of his presence in the middle of the battle as a "terrible mistake." As the bloody battle progresses, a large group of enemy soldiers open fire on Charley's group: "It was like a blade cutting grain. He heard the bullets hitting the men—little *thunk-slaps*—and saw the men falling. Some of them screamed as they fell. Most were silent. Many were dead before they hit the ground. Many were torn apart, hit ten or twelve or more times before they had time to drop." At one point, two bullets even smash together directly in front of him and hit the ground in one twisted chunk of metal. "That sight was more horrifying than the death he'd seen," wrote Paulsen. "How many bullets, he thought, would have to be flying around for two of them to collide in midair?"

The Union forces eventually fall back in retreat. Charley manages to reach safety in nearby woods, but he is so shaken by his experience that he vomits and finds himself questioning how God could permit such savagery. The following day, Union commanders organize the troops for another charge against the Confederate forces. When the Union army marches past the corpses of soldiers slain the previous day, young Charley sees that many of the dead soldiers are wearing red flannel shirts, which marks them as natives of Minnesota.

Soldiers sit at a bridge near the site of the Battle of Bull Run in Virginia in 1862.
Courtesy of the National Archives and Records Administration.

As Charley continues on, he becomes convinced he is going to die. But he is spared a second day of fighting when the Northern troops discover that the enemy withdrew from the area during the night.

Charley's first exposure to the brutal reality of war has a devastating emotional impact on him. Over the next few weeks, he becomes convinced that he will soon die on the battlefield. "He could not live," wrote Paulsen. "Many others would die with him and many would live but he knew one thing: He would die. In the next battle or the one after that or the one after that he would die."

A short time later, Charley's company is sent to another battle in Virginia. Just before going into battle, he talks with a young soldier named Nelson. He has never been in combat before, but he talks confidently of whipping the Confederates and ignores Charley's warnings about the true nature of war. Charley and his comrades are then sent into battle.

When the rebel troops (Confederates) break into flight, Charley chases after them at full speed, overcome with a crazy desire to kill all Confederate soldiers before they can kill him. A Union sergeant stops him and orders him back to camp. But as Charley walks back through the battlefield, he encounters Nelson. He sees that Nelson has been shot in the stomach, which means that he is doomed to die. He knows that soldiers with stomach wounds were always left on the battlefield because surgeons could not treat their wounds.

Charley kneels down next to Nelson and tries to comfort him. During their short conversation, the wounded soldier asks Charley to load his rifle for him in case the enemy returns. Charley obliges with tears in his eyes, because he knows that the young soldier is preparing to shoot himself to spare himself a slow and painful death. Charley finally leaves Nelson and begins the long walk back to camp. As he walks on, he hears a single rifle shot behind him.

Charley spends the next three months in an army camp. As time passes, the weather turns colder and deadly diseases sweep through the camp. During this period, Charley decides that "it was every man for himself. He became adept at camp survival. He pulled his own weight, took his turn gathering food and wood, and cleaning, and cooking, but he made a private world for himself where he kept his thoughts and knowledge. . . . He did not like to look at people as much as he once did. He did not like to learn about them. It was better if he didn't know them, become too friendly with them. They died so fast."

One night, Charley is assigned guard duty down by a nearby river. In the middle of the night, he strikes up a conversation with an unseen Confederate soldier on the other side of the river. As the night wears on, the two young men even arrange to trade coffee for tobacco by throwing a rope across the river. As they talk, they learn that they are both young farmers with very similar backgrounds. The rebel soldier reacts bitterly to this discovery, noting that the next day they might still find themselves shooting at one another.

A short time later, Charley and several other soldiers are ordered to kill some captured horses to provide meat for the camp's sick soldiers. This order, writes Paulsen, "put him on the edge of mutiny. He had been raised with workhorses

A horse lies dead on a Gettysburg battlefield.
Courtesy of the Library of Congress.

and had come to love them. Killing the horses—watching them drop as they were shot in the head—made him almost physically ill."

Charley then takes part in his third major battle, in Maryland. During this clash, Charley's company faces a rebel cavalry charge. As the cavalry draw into shooting range, the Union troops are ordered to shoot the horses that the Confederates are riding. The volley of rifle fire virtually destroys the rebel charge: "The result was devastating. Charley held [aimed] high and took a trooper full in the chest, but most of the other men held on the horses and not one animal came through unhit. In a great cloud they went down, somersaulting, rolling over the troopers on their backs, breaking themselves and the men; and the screams—the screams of the wounded horses hit by soft, large-caliber expanding bullets, horses with heads blown open, horses with jaws shot away, horses with eyes shot out or with intestines dangling in their hooves, horses torn and dying—screamed louder than a thousand, louder than a million men."

The battle continued throughout the day and into the evening. As darkness began to fall over the battlefield, "Charley became a madman. He attacked anything and everything that came into his range—slashing, clubbing, hammering, jabbing, cutting—and always screaming, screaming in fear, in anger and finally in a kind of rabid, insane joy." When he returns to the Union encampment, he is so covered with blood that his fellow soldiers think he has been wounded. They send Charley to the hospital tent, where he sees a pile of amputated arms and legs that stands four feet high and more than ten feet long. He also sees another huge pile of dead bodies. After waiting in the freezing cold for a while, he is examined by a doctor. It turns out that he is not wounded, but before he can return to his unit, a doctor stops him. The surgeon orders him to help create a windbreak out of the bodies of the dead soldiers so that he can protect his hands from the freezing wind. By the time this horrible task is completed, Charley and another soldier have created a wall of dead men five feet high and thirty feet long.

The novel then follows Charley to the famous Battle of Gettysburg in Pennsylvania. During this battle, Confederate forces mount a desperate charge across an open meadow to reach Union troops that are protected by a large stone wall. As the rebels charge forward, Northern cannons and rifles rip the soldiers apart. "The Confederates had to march through a storm of fire and Charley lay and watched them and nearly felt sorry for them. They were so brave, he thought—or foolish. They kept coming, even when thousands of them were down and dying." Most of the rebels are killed or wounded before they can reach the stone wall, but a few make it. Charley and the other members of the First Minnesota Volunteers rush forward to meet these attackers. During this fierce and bloody combat, Charley is wounded and loses consciousness.

The last chapter of *Soldier's Heart* takes place in June 1867, more than two years after the war ended. Charley is using a cane to walk along a quiet river. He carries a picnic sack in his free hand. As he walks, he recalls the earliest days of the war, when he was a part of a parade, flanked by cheering children and pretty girls waving flags. He recalls those memories as "sweet" and "pretty." When he reaches a peaceful spot along the riverbank, he painfully seats himself and takes out his

Soldiers from both the Union and the Confederacy lie dead on the Gettysburg battlefield in July 1863.
Photograph by Timothy H. O'Sullivan. Courtesy of the National Archives and Records Administration.

lunch. He also takes out a loaded revolver that he took from the body of a Confederate officer during the war. He thinks about how "pretty" the pistol is, and about how easy it would be to raise the pistol to his head and pull the trigger. But then he puts the gun down and watches the river pass by, thinking again "of all the pretty things."

Style and themes in *Soldier's Heart*

In *Soldier's Heart,* Paulsen writes from the perspective of one young, sensitive soldier to show how war can destroy not only the bodies but also the minds of its participants. As the author noted in his foreword, "Even for those who survive—and the vast majority of soldiers who go to war *do* survive—the mental damage done is often permanent. What they have seen and been forced to do is frequently so horrific and devastating that it simply cannot be tolerated by the human psyche [mind and spirit]."

This type of emotional injury is now known as post-traumatic stress disorder or post-traumatic stress syndrome. But in the Civil War, states Paulsen, "the syndrome was generally not recognized at all. . . . In those days, there was no scientific knowledge of mental disorders and no effort was made to help the men who were damaged. Some men came through combat unscathed [without emotional damage]. Most did not. These men were somehow different from other men. They were said to have soldier's heart."

Paulsen uses a straightforward writing style to explore how war can change a person's personality and outlook on life. The author moves chronologically through Charley's life, beginning with his enlistment and continuing through each of his battlefield experiences. As the novel progresses, Paulsen shows how the war is killing Charley's spirit with each passing day. Paulsen then concludes with a final chapter that reveals that more than two years after the war's end, Charley still carries crippling physical and emotional wounds. In fact, a part of him looks forward to dying, even though he is only twenty-one years old. He thinks that death will reunite him with fallen army comrades and enable him to escape war memories that continue to haunt him. The grim conclusion of *Soldier's Heart* shows that even soldiers who survive wars are forever changed by their wartime experiences.

Research and Activity Ideas

1) During the course of the novel, Charley withdraws from the other soldiers in his company. He avoids making friends with anyone and keeps to himself. Why do you think he does this?

2) Charley witnesses the violent deaths of horses in two separate incidents. When he is forced to shoot captured horses to provide food for sick men, he is pushed to the edge of mutiny. Later, he describes a Confederate cavalry charge that is stopped by a volley of rifle fire directed at the cavalry's mounts. According to Charley, the screams of the wounded horses sound "louder than a million men." Why do you think the deaths of the horses in these two cases bothered Charley so much?

3) *Soldier's Heart* contains many graphic scenes of violence on the battlefield. But the author also includes numerous

other post-battle images that show the horrors of war, such as the wall of corpses that Charley must help build to protect the army surgeon from the wind. What other non-combat images in *Soldier's Heart* show the awful toll of war? Which images particularly seem to bother Charley? Do they contribute to the "soldier's heart" that he has developed by the end of the novel?

4) Charley is only fifteen years old when he takes part in his first battle. Do you know anyone—a brother or sister or cousin or friend—of about that age? How do you think he or she would react if placed in Charley's situation?

Related Titles

Beatty, Patricia. *Charley Skedaddle*. New York: Morrow, 1987. *A novel about a twelve-year-old boy from New York City who joins the Union Army as a drummer, then deserts his unit after realizing the horrors of combat.*

Kovic, Ron. *Born on the Fourth of July*. New York: McGraw-Hill, 1976. *The true story of a patriotic young American who was eager to join the army and fight in Vietnam, but then experiences the reality of war and returns home a disabled and disillusioned veteran.*

Whitman, Walt. "The Wound Dresser." Originally published in 1892. Included in multiple editions of *Leaves of Grass*. *A poem about the tragic consequences of war, based on Whitman's experiences helping wounded soldiers during the Civil War.*

Where to Learn More About . . .

Gary Paulsen and *Soldier's Heart*

Collier, Laurie, and Joyce Nakamura. *Major Authors and Illustrators for Young Adults*. Detroit: Gale Research, 1993.

"Gary Paulsen's Biography." *Scholastic.com*. [Online] http://www2.scholastic.com/teachers/authorsandbooks/authorstudies/authorhome.jhtml?authorID=71&collateralID=5258&displayName=Biography (accessed on August 20, 2001).

Paulsen, Gary. *Eastern Sun, Winter Moon: An Autobiographical Odyssey*. New York: Delacorte Books, 1993.

Paulsen, Gary. *Guts: The True Stories Behind Hatchet and the Brian Books*. New York: Delacorte Books, 2001.

Random House. *Gary Paulsen*. [Online] http://www.randomhouse.com/features/garypaulsen (accessed on August 20, 2001).

Salvner, Gary M. *Presenting Gary Paulsen*. New York: Twayne, 1996.

Something About the Author, vol. 54. Detroit: Gale Research, 1989.

Civil War Soldiers and Their Wartime Experiences

McPherson, James. *For Cause and Comrades: Why Men Fought in the Civil War.* New York: Oxford University Press, 1997.

Meltzer, Milton, ed. *Voices from the Civil War: A Documentary History of the Great American Conflict.* New York: Crowell, 1989.

Mitchell, Reid. *Civil War Soldiers: Their Expectations and Their Experiences.* New York: Viking Press, 1988.

Moe, Richard. *The Last Full Measure: The Life and Death of the First Minnesota Volunteers.* New York: Avon, 1994.

Shotwell, Randolph Abbott. *Papers.* Raleigh, NC: North Carolina Historical Commission, 1929–31.

The Tamarack Tree

Written by Patricia Clapp

The Tamarack Tree tells the story of Rosemary Leigh, an English teenager who arrives in the United States in 1859, just before the start of the American Civil War (1861–65). Rosemary lives in Vicksburg, Mississippi, where she grows to love the kindness and hospitality of the Southern people and culture. At the same time, though, Rosemary cannot understand the practice of slavery and thinks it is wrong for her friends to own other human beings. She struggles with her mixed emotions as the war approaches her new home.

Much of the action in *The Tamarack Tree* takes place during the siege of Vicksburg in 1863. At this time, Union forces surrounded the city to prevent supplies from entering and pounded it with artillery fire for nearly two months. Rosemary describes the terrible fear and hunger experienced by the residents of Vicksburg during the siege.

Biography of author Patricia Clapp

Patricia Clapp was born on June 9, 1912, in Boston, Massachusetts, to Howard and Elizabeth Clapp. She attended the Columbia University School of Journalism at the age of twenty and also took various writing courses over the years. She married Edward della Torre Cone in 1933. They eventually had three children, Christopher, Patricia, and Pamela.

Clapp has said that she considers herself mostly a "theater person." She was active in community theater for over forty years, writing and directing plays. Beginning in the 1950s, she also published numerous plays for children and young adults. She first tried her hand at writing historical fiction in the late 1960s. Her first young adult novel, *Constance: A Story of Early Plymouth,* was published in 1968. The book was a runner-up for the National Book Award for Children's Literature and won the Lewis Carroll Shelf Award.

Clapp used the Civil War as the subject of her historical novel *The Tamarack Tree,* published in 1986. This book tells the story of Rosemary Leigh, a young woman who moves from England to Vicksburg, Mississippi, at the start of the Civil War. Rosemary lives through the siege of Vicksburg in 1863, when Union troops under General Ulysses S. Grant (1822–1885) surrounded the city and attacked it with cannons for forty-seven days. The siege caused terrible hardships and near starvation for many of the city's residents.

In *Contemporary Authors,* Clapp said that she enjoys writing historical fiction because she believes in old-fashioned values, like "good manners, thoughtfulness, kindness, and those outmoded beautiful words 'ladies' and 'gentlemen.'" The author lives in Upper Montclair, New Jersey.

Historical background of *The Tamarack Tree*

The events in *The Tamarack Tree* take place during the Civil War. This was a conflict between the Northern part of the United States, known as the Union, and the Southern half of the country, known as the Confederacy. For many years before the war began in 1861, the two sides argued bitterly over several issues, including slavery.

Many people in the North believed that slavery was wrong and wanted to outlaw the practice. But the South's economy depended on slavery, and white Southerners argued that the national government should not interfere with their traditional way of life. When it became clear that the two sides could not reach an agreement, several Southern states seceded (withdrew) from the United States and formed their own country that allowed slavery, called the Confederate States of America, or the Confederacy. But Northern political leaders were determined not to let the Southern states leave the Union without a fight.

The Civil War lasted for four long years and took the lives of over six hundred thousand Americans. Most of the fighting took place in the South. One of the Union's main strategies involved taking control of the entire length of the Mississippi River. This major waterway flows south from Minnesota all the way to the Gulf of Mexico. Union leaders believed that controlling the Mississippi would help them to transport troops and supplies into the South. They also knew that it would divide the Confederate states west of the river (Texas, Arkansas, and Louisiana) from those east of the river.

The main obstacle to the Union's plan to control the Mississippi River was the city of Vicksburg, Mississippi. Vicksburg is located on top of high bluffs along the river's eastern shoreline. During the Civil War, the Confederates placed cannons and troops in the bluffs above the river to protect the city from a naval attack. Since Vicksburg was so well-defended, Union forces ended up capturing most of the length of the river before they turned their attention to Vicksburg. The city became the last major Confederate stronghold on the mighty Mississippi.

In May 1862, Admiral David Farragut (1801–1870) brought the Union navy up to the city from the South. The ships fired on Vicksburg for several weeks, but they soon decided it would be impossible to capture the city from the river alone. Clapp mentions this early firing of artillery shells in *The Tamarack Tree*. Rosemary's house is hit, but she survives because her brother had the good sense to dig a cave in their yard. They end up moving to a mansion higher in the hills at this point in the story.

By the end of 1862, Union forces had taken control of the entire Mississippi River except for two hundred miles below Vicksburg. Then Union general Ulysses S. Grant came up with a brilliant and daring plan to capture the city. In early 1863, Grant brought thirty-three thousand troops down the Louisiana side of the river, through a maze of swamps and

The siege of Vicksburg.
Lithograph, original copyright 1888 by Kurz & Allison, Art Publishers, Chicago, Illinois. Courtesy of the Library of Congress.

marshes. In late April, they met up with a fleet of Union ships and were transported to the Mississippi side. The Union forces won a number of minor battles in the countryside around Vicksburg over the next few weeks. By mid-May, Grant had surrounded the city. By this time, reinforcements had increased his numbers to seventy thousand men. In contrast, there were only thirty thousand Confederate troops under General John C. Pemberton (1814–1881) in Vicksburg. At this point, Grant decided to set up a siege of Vicksburg. This strategy involves surrounding a target and preventing supplies from entering. Grant hoped that the siege would starve the city into surrendering.

During the siege of Vicksburg, constant artillery fire forced many residents to leave their homes and hide in caves on the outskirts of town. Food supplies decreased until people were near starvation. In fact, some people were forced to eat rats and mules in order to survive. There was also a shortage of medical supplies to treat the growing number of wounded sol-

diers and civilians (people who are not part of the army, including women and children). Conditions became so grim in Vicksburg that some people had nervous breakdowns. In *The Tamarack Tree*, Rosemary lives through the siege of Vicksburg. She becomes very hungry herself and sees other people near starvation. She also witnesses the damage from artillery fire and helps treat wounded soldiers. Her friend Ben Fraser, who is a Confederate soldier, has a nervous breakdown due to fear and hunger.

The siege of Vicksburg lasted for forty-seven days, from May to July 1863. On June 28, a large group of Confederate soldiers sent a note to Pemberton asking him to surrender. "If you can't feed us, you had better surrender, horrible as the idea is, than suffer this noble army to disgrace themselves by desertion," the note warned. "This army is now ripe for mutiny, unless it can be fed." Pemberton finally surrendered on July 4. As soon as Vicksburg fell, Union soldiers began sharing their food with the city's starving people. A few days later, Union

Starving citizens of New Orleans, Louisiana, gather to be fed by Union soldiers.
Illustration originally published in Harper's Weekly *in 1862.
Courtesy of the Library of Congress.*

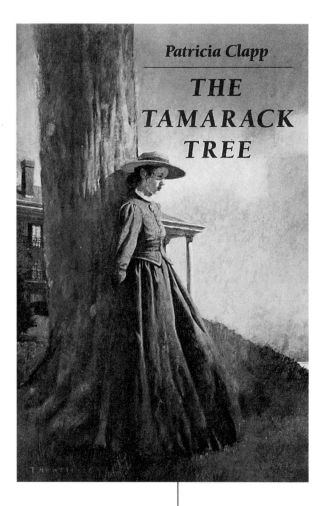

Cover of *The Tamarack Tree*.
Designed by Troy Howell.
Reproduced by permission of
HarperCollins Publishers.

forces captured the nearby city of Port Hudson, Louisiana, to gain control over the entire length of the Mississippi River.

Grant's grim victory in Vicksburg shook the confidence of the Confederacy. It happened about the same time as another important Union victory at the Battle of Gettysburg in Pennsylvania. The combination of these two events changed the way both sides viewed the war. People in the South felt discouraged and began to worry that they might lose. People in the North felt encouraged and became more determined to press on for a complete victory. These impressive Union victories also helped President Abraham Lincoln (1809–1865) get reelected in 1864, as voters gained confidence in him and his war policies.

Plot and characters of *The Tamarack Tree*

The story in *The Tamarack Tree* is told from the perspective of Rosemary Leigh. Rosemary was born in England. Her father, who was a doctor, died when she was twelve. A year later, her mother died after a long illness, leaving her an orphan. At the age of fourteen, Rosemary moves to the United States to live with her older brother, Derek Leigh. Derek lives in Vicksburg, Mississippi, where he works as an apprentice at the law firm of their uncle, William Stafford.

Rosemary arrives at the port of New Orleans, where the Mississippi River flows into the Gulf of Mexico, in the summer of 1859. At this time, tension is increasing between the Northern and the Southern parts of the United States. One of the main points of disagreement between the two halves of the country is slavery. Rosemary sees black people for the first time when she reaches New Orleans. She learns about the practice of slavery and immediately dislikes the idea.

Rosemary and her brother take a steamship up the Mississippi River to Vicksburg. As she approaches her new home, Rosemary notices that the city is perched on top of high bluffs overlooking the river. She is impressed by the busy port, which sends shipments of cotton all over the world. Rosemary and Derek soon settle into a small, comfortable house. They hire a free black woman named Amanda to work as their housekeeper. Her husband, Hector, works for Uncle Will's law firm. Their young daughter, Betsy, comes with Amanda to Rosemary's house every day. Amanda teaches Rosemary a great deal about cooking and being a good hostess.

Shortly after Rosemary settles in, she receives a visit from Mary Byrd Blair. Mary Byrd is a young woman about Rosemary's age. She was born and raised on a plantation outside of Vicksburg. She comes from a wealthy family that owns many slaves. Mary Byrd is a pleasant, talkative Southern belle whose life revolves around social events and shopping trips. She also enjoys flirting with young men, including Derek. She and Rosemary soon become close friends.

Knowing that the Blair family owns slaves, Rosemary asks Mary Byrd how she feels about slavery. Her answer shows the attitude of many white Southerners during the Civil War era: "Why we all *love* our people, Rosemary. Of course I don't see much of ours; they're way out on our plantation at Champion Hill. But my daddy builds cabins for them, and he says they sing while they're working, and they're happy folks! Whatever would they do if we didn't look out for them? I know Northerners think it's wrong to have slaves, but they don't understand how it is in the South. The slaves and the plantation owners—well, they need each other to get along. It's like children, my daddy says. Parents see after their children, but the children must do as they're told."

Despite her friend's explanation of the Southern point of view, Rosemary still believes that slavery is wrong. She cannot accept the idea of owning other people. When she tells Derek how she feels about the issue, he responds: "That is the way the northern part of the United States feels: that it is wrong to buy or sell human beings; that if anyone, black or white, works for a living he should be paid for his work, just like we pay Amanda. And there you have the two sides of the slavery coin, Tad [Derek's nickname for Rosemary]. The North feels it is exploiting people who have no choice, the South considering it natural and desirable."

In 1861, on her sixteenth birthday, Rosemary meets Jeffrey Howard. He is from Boston, Massachusetts, where he is a student at Harvard University. He is in Vicksburg visiting Rosemary's uncle. Jeff calls on Rosemary often in the next few weeks. When the Civil War begins, however, he decides to return to the North in order to join the Union army. Rosemary argues with him about this decision. She does not want anything bad to happen to Jeff, and she also cannot picture him marching back to Vicksburg and fighting against her friends.

Rosemary feels torn by the war. She does not approve of slavery, but she likes the South and all the people she has met there. "Since Derek brought me to Vicksburg," she tells Jeff, "people have been so kind. Courteous—and helpful—and hospitable. They have made us feel liked—and *wanted*. Most of these people are slave owners. They buy and sell human beings like—like furniture! Perhaps, as I have been told, they are kind and caring to their . . . property, but men and women are not property! Should not be! Must not be! Is it just because God gave some human beings black skin that white men do not regard them as *people*? Oh, Jeff, I don't know what to think! Sometimes I feel as if I were split right down the middle."

During the first year of the war, Rosemary is surprised to find that her life in Vicksburg goes on as usual. She hears about the battles that take place between Union and Confederate forces, but they do not affect her yet. On her seventeenth birthday, Rosemary meets Benjamin Blair Fraser. Ben is a cousin of Mary Byrd and a soldier in the Confederate army. He calls on Rosemary any time he can get away from his duties. As the war drags on, Rosemary begins to notice a shortage of basic goods. The shops in town no longer carry fresh fruits or vegetables, fabric, buttons, paper, and other things that she had taken for granted before. The shortages occur because the Union navy has set up blockades of Southern ports to prevent shipments of goods from getting in. The North used this strategy to make it more difficult for the Confederate army to get supplies from overseas. At first, Rosemary and the other residents of Vicksburg make do with food collected from the plantations outside town. But this supply soon begins running low as well.

In the spring of 1862, the war finally approaches Vicksburg. Rosemary sees Union ships sailing up the Mississippi River, just out of range of the Confederate guns protecting the city. Most people thought that Vicksburg was safe from a Union attack since its position on a high bluff made it easy to defend. But Derek knows that Vicksburg is an important target if the Union plans to take control of the entire Mississippi River. He decides to dig a cave in the side of a hill in their yard. He tells Rosemary that they will sleep in the cave if the city comes under attack.

Around this time, Rosemary hears the story of how her housekeeper's husband came to America. Hector is from Liberia, a country on the west coast of Africa. Liberia was established as a colony where Americans who opposed slavery could send blacks to live as free people. Early in the debate over slavery, some people believed that blacks would never be considered the equals of whites in the United States. They felt that racism would always exist and limit the rights of African Americans. They argued that the best way to solve this problem was to return blacks to a special colony in Africa. This idea was known as "colonization."

Hector tells Rosemary about Simon, his friend growing up in Liberia. Simon's grandfather was an African prince. But the prince was captured in a war with a neighboring tribe and sold to white traders who took him to America. The prince lived in the United States for fifty years in terrible conditions of slavery. He finally made it back to Africa, but he died a few months later. Hector met the prince and was very impressed by him. He also learned that there were people in the United States who worked to free slaves. "The more I heard that word 'slave,' the more I hated it," Hector recalls. "And Simon told me about people who tried to help some of the slaves escape to places where they could be free folks. And somehow I knew that was what I had to do. Get myself to America, to where the slaves were, and find ways to help them get free."

On May 26, 1862, Union ships begin firing upon Vicksburg (see box). A few days later, an artillery shell hits the house while Rosemary and Derek are in the cave. They move to a mansion higher up in the hills. As it turns out, the mansion has served as a station on the Underground Railroad—a network of homes and farms where slaves could go for help in

A Resident Remembers the Siege of Vicksburg

In *The Tamarack Tree,* Rosemary's description of life in Vicksburg during the siege is very realistic. Many similar details are included in an unknown Northern woman's diary of the siege of Vicksburg. The following excerpt from the diary appears in Milton Meltzer's book *Voices from the Civil War:*

> We are utterly cut off from the world, surrounded by a circle of fire. Would it be wise like the scorpion to sting ourselves to death? The fiery shower of shells goes on day and night. . . . People do nothing but eat what they can get, sleep when they can, and dodge the shells. There are three intervals when the shelling stops, either for the guns to cool or for the gunners' meals, I suppose—about eight in the morning, the same in the evening, and at noon. In that time we have both to prepare and eat ours. . . . At all the caves I could see from my high perch, people were sitting, eating their poor suppers at the cave doors, ready to plunge in again. As the first shell again flew they dived, and not a human being was visible. . . . I think all the dogs and cats must be killed or starved; we don't see any more pitiful animals prowling around.

escaping to the North. A secret tunnel in the cellar leads hundreds of yards into some woods. Rosemary soon learns that Hector helped dig the tunnel, and that both Derek and Uncle Will were involved in the Underground Railroad.

The shelling of Vicksburg ends after a few weeks. Before long, however, Rosemary begins hearing about battles that are taking place not far from the city. Union forces under General Ulysses S. Grant claim a series of victories in the surrounding countryside over the next several months. After one of these battles, the Blair plantation at Champion Hill is burned and many of their slaves escape. By May 1863, Northern forces have surrounded Vicksburg. Grant decides to set up a siege of the city in hopes of starving the Confederate forces into surrendering. In the meantime, he also resumes shelling the city from the river.

Rosemary describes the hardships Vicksburg residents suffer during the siege. The most critical problem is the lack of food. Grant's forces have destroyed or cut off access to the plantations that used to provide some food, and people slowly begin starving. The situation is even worse for the troops, who must live on official rations. Every morning, several Confederate soldiers show up at the back door of the mansion while Amanda is making cornbread and beg her to let them lick the bowl. Rosemary sees Ben Fraser during the siege, and he is very thin and tired.

Looking for a way to help, Rosemary, Derek, and Mary Byrd volunteer to treat wounded soldiers in a makeshift hospital. Rosemary is shocked at the terrible conditions there. They have no medical supplies or clean water to give the soldiers because the siege has cut off all supplies. "When we stepped through the door of an abandoned warehouse it was like walking into a nightmare," she says. "Twenty or so cots were pushed close together, all of them filled, as were mattresses, pallets, and blankets laid on the floor. The smell of blood and vomit so permeated [filled] the place I could scarcely breathe."

One day, Rosemary finds Ben Fraser among the wounded soldiers. He survives his wound, but he is terrified and ends up deserting the army (leaving illegally before his term of service has ended). The fear, hunger, and fatigue finally cause Ben to have a nervous breakdown. He dies shortly after the city of Vicksburg surrenders on July 4, 1863. Rosemary remembers how the city looked when the siege finally ended: "Everywhere were houses and empty shops, either entirely demolished or badly damaged. Scarcely a windowpane remained. In places great trees had fallen, their leaves and splintered limbs stretching over yards of ground. The green hillside was filled with craters where shells had landed. The proud city of Vicksburg had been through a siege, and the scars would show for years."

As soon as Vicksburg surrenders, the Union army provides food and supplies for the starving people. Rosemary is impressed with how professionally the Northern soldiers behave. They simply march in to take control of the city, with no gloating or celebration. Rosemary is surprised to see Jeff Howard among the Union forces marching through Vicksburg. She allows him to call on her, and they fall in love. In the meantime, Derek tells Rosemary that he loves Mary Byrd and wants to marry her. But before he can propose, Mary Byrd finds out that Derek helped slaves escape on the Underground Rail-

Union general Ulysses S. Grant stands in camp during the Civil War. *Courtesy of the National Archives and Records Administration.*

road. She considers this a betrayal and calls him a traitor to the Southern cause. But Derek refuses to apologize for his actions and tells her that he always believed slavery was wrong. Mary Byrd says that they come from different cultures and asks him to leave.

At this point, Derek and Rosemary decide to return to England. When Rosemary goes to say goodbye to Mary Byrd, she finds that her friend has done some thinking. The events of the war have forced Mary Byrd to reconsider some of the ideas and attitudes she has held since birth. The Blairs have lost most of their money and property, including their slaves. Mary Byrd has learned that it was actually the slaves of another plantation owner who burned down her family's plantation, rather than the Union forces. As the Northern troops approached, these slaves killed their master—who had treated them cruelly—and escaped. Then they wandered across the countryside doing as much damage to whites' property as they could.

Mary Byrd was shocked to hear that some people were mean to their slaves. She never realized that black people were not happy with their lives under slavery. "And so I began to see what a fairy tale I had lived in. Everything isn't always rosy and happy the way I thought it was—thought it would always be," she admits. "You see, Rosemary, I never knew those slaves needed help. They were just—there. Had always been. And I thought they *wanted* to be." Once Mary Byrd understands the true nature of slavery, she and Derek make up. They get married and leave for London with Rosemary. Jeff Howard plans to join them when his service in the Union army ends.

As she sets sail for England, Rosemary insists that she is glad she came to the United States, despite the hardships caused by the Civil War. When Derek says he should never have brought her to Vicksburg, she says, "And denied me the chance to learn more about the world? About America? About people? People with strong beliefs, who are willing to fight for them? I think I would be a lesser person now, if that had happened."

Style and themes in *The Tamarack Tree*

The Tamarack Tree is written in the style of a diary. The main character, Rosemary Leigh, tells the story. In the first chapter, Rosemary introduces herself and tells the reader that she is writing in her diary as a way to keep her mind occupied. She is in the middle of the siege of Vicksburg, and she does not want to think about the danger that surrounds her. The remaining chapters are organized chronologically by date. Rosemary starts out by remembering her arrival in America in 1859 and her introduction to Southern culture. She recalls the beginning of the Civil War in 1861 and talks about some of the issues behind the conflict. The main action of the story takes place when Rosemary describes her experiences during the siege of Vicksburg in 1863. The final chapters bring the reader up to date on what happens after the first chapter was written, when the siege of Vicksburg ends.

Author Patricia Clapp probably chose to tell the story from Rosemary's point of view because she is an outsider. Since she is from England, Rosemary does not have strong opinions about the issues that divide the United States at the time she arrives in America. She is able to remain objective and see both sides of the story. For example, Rosemary disagrees with the practice of slavery and thinks it is wrong for people to own other people. But she also feels great friendship and loyalty toward the people of Vicksburg, many of whom own slaves. Rosemary can understand Mary Byrd's belief that her father was actually helping his slaves by giving them food, housing, and medical care in exchange for their work on his plantation. But she can also understand Hector's hatred of slavery and his lifelong mission to help slaves escape. By presenting the issues from an outsider's point of view, Clapp helps readers see both sides as well.

One of the main themes of *The Tamarack Tree* is that people who supported the Confederate side during the Civil War were not necessarily evil. Many Southerners, like the residents of Vicksburg, were simply fighting to defend their homes and families. Some Southerners were fighting to preserve the institution of slavery. But many of those who owned slaves, like Mary Byrd, did so out of misguided ideas about tradition and racial differences rather than from a desire to treat black people cruelly. Rosemary makes many friends during her years in Vicksburg. Through her, the reader comes to know and like several characters who support the Confederate cause. As Rosemary describes the hardships that she and other residents of the city suffer during the siege, the reader feels some sympathy for the people of the South.

Another major theme in *The Tamarack Tree* involves a young woman discovering her own courage and determination under difficult conditions. When Rosemary arrives in the United States at the age of fourteen, she has led a relatively sheltered life. She must adapt to a new culture and learn how to run a household. She also attracts the attention of young men for the first time. Shortly after her arrival, Rosemary finds herself trapped in the middle of a war that has nothing to do with her. She struggles to understand and form her own opinions about the issues behind the conflict. Once the siege of Vicksburg begins, Rosemary is forced to face the horrors of war. She hides from the constant shelling, suffers from shortages of food and other basic supplies, and treats wounded soldiers in a field hospital. Through all her experiences in the United States, Rosemary learns many things and becomes stronger and more independent. At the end of the novel, she recognizes that the hardships she has suffered have made her a better person.

Research and Activity Ideas

1) If Rosemary Leigh had to choose one side or the other, do you think she would support the Union or the Confederacy? Why? Provide details from the book to support your answer.

2) Compare Mary Byrd's view of slavery with Hector's view of slavery. What aspects of their backgrounds have made them feel the way they do?

3) Look at a map of the United States. Why was Vicksburg such an important target for Union forces? Why was the city so difficult to capture? Trace the route Union general Ulysses S. Grant used to position his troops in a circle around Vicksburg in order to lay siege to the city.

4) Grant's siege of Vicksburg has been criticized because it harmed the civilian residents of the city as well as the Confederate soldiers who were defending it. Think about what Rosemary and her friends went through during the siege. How do you feel about Grant's decision to fight the war in this way?

Related Titles

Beatty, Patricia. *Who Comes with Cannons?* New York: Morrow Junior Books, 1992. *A novel about a twelve-year-old Quaker girl living with relatives in North Carolina who run a station on the Underground Railroad.*

Chang, Ina. *A Separate Battle: Women in the Civil War.* New York: Lodestar Books, 1991. Reprint, New York: Puffin Books, 1996. *A nonfiction book about the hardships of the home front and the contributions of women on both sides of the Civil War.*

Rinaldi, Ann. *Amelia's War.* New York: Scholastic Press, 1999. *A novel based on an actual incident in which a Maryland town was divided over which side to support in the Civil War.*

Wisler, G. Clifton. *The Drummer Boy of Vicksburg.* New York: Lodestar Books, 1997. *A novel based on the life of a real drummer boy in the Union Army who served in the siege of Vicksburg.*

Where to Learn More About . . .

Patricia Clapp and *The Tamarack Tree*

Contemporary Authors, New Revision Series. Vol. 37. Detroit: Gale, 1992.

General Ulysses S. Grant and the Siege of Vicksburg

Grant, Ulysses S. *Personal Memoirs of U. S. Grant.* New York: C. L. Webster & Co., 1885. Reprint, New York: Penguin Books, 1999.

Macdonald, John. *Great Battles of the Civil War.* New York: Macmillan, 1988.

McFeely, William S. *Grant: A Biography.* New York: Norton, 1981.

Meltzer, Milton, ed. *Voices from the Civil War: A Documentary History of the Great American Conflict.* New York: Crowell, 1989.

With Every Drop of Blood

Written by James Lincoln Collier and Christopher Collier

With *Every Drop of Blood* tells the story of Johnny, a fourteen-year-old farm boy from the Shenandoah Valley region of Virginia. This area was the site of several important campaigns (connected series of military operations) during the American Civil War (1861–65). After his father is killed in the fighting, Johnny wants to get revenge and to help the Confederate cause. He joins a wagon train carrying supplies to Confederate troops defending the capital city of Richmond. But the wagon train is attacked by Union soldiers, and Johnny is captured. He is shocked to see that the Union soldier who captured him, Cush Turner, is a black boy about his own age. The novel follows the growing friendship between Johnny and Cush during the final days of the Civil War.

With Every Drop of Blood was written by James Lincoln Collier (1928–) and Christopher Collier (1930–). This team of brothers has worked together to write several historical novels for young adults. Although the characters of Johnny and Cush never really existed, the Colliers based their story on actual events that took place in the Shenandoah Valley during the Civil War. The novel contains several battle scenes and some mild cursing. It also includes offensive terms for African Americans. The authors explain their decision to use such terms in a preface to the book. Their research showed that white people living in the Shenandoah Valley during the mid-1800s would have used these terms to refer to blacks. They felt that they needed to include the terms in their novel in order to present their characters in a historically accurate manner.

Biographies of James Lincoln Collier and Christopher Collier

With Every Drop of Blood was written by brothers James Lincoln Collier and Christopher Collier. James is a writer who has published dozens of books for young adults. Christopher is a history professor. They have worked together to write several books of historical fiction, including the award-winning novel *My Brother Sam Is Dead*.

James Lincoln Collier was born on June 27, 1928. Christopher Collier was born on January 29, 1930. Their parents were Edmund and Katharine (Brown) Collier. They grew up in Connecticut. As a boy, James was inspired by the many members of his family who made their livings as writers. He said in the *Fifth Book of Junior Authors and Illustrators* that he "became a writer the way other young people go into the family business. It never occurred to me that I couldn't write; it was what people did, and it has been what I have done since I became an adult."

James graduated from Hamilton College in 1950. After serving in the army during the Korean War (1950–53), he became a freelance writer. He has published hundreds of articles in magazines over the years as well as many books for adults. He has also written a number of books for children and young adults. James has always loved music and plays the trombone professionally. Many of his books center around musicians and jazz.

Christopher Collier became interested in history at an early age. When he was fourteen, he read *They Also Ran* by Irving Stone (1903–1989). This book told about all the losing presidential candidates through U.S. history. "That is the first history I recall reading for fun, but ever since then I have made the study of history my principal concern," he said in *Contemporary Authors*.

Christopher graduated from Clark University in Massachusetts in 1951. After serving in the U.S. Army for two years, he returned to college. He earned a master's degree from Columbia University in 1955 and a doctorate in 1964. He taught history in public schools for several years in the late 1950s and then became a college history professor. He has taught at the University of Connecticut since 1984. He has also been Connecticut's state historian since 1985.

"It was when I was teaching eighth-grade American history that I was inspired to write historical novels," Christopher Collier said in *Contemporary Authors*. "Surely there must be a better—more interesting and memorable—way to teach such exciting stuff as history is made of than through the dull, dull textbooks we used." By this time, his brother James had already published several novels for young adults. After years of trying, Christopher finally convinced him that they should work together to write historical fiction.

James Lincoln Collier (left) and Christopher Collier, authors of *With Every Drop of Blood*. *Reproduced by permission of Christopher Collier.*

The Collier brothers published their first book together in 1974. *My Brother Sam Is Dead* takes place during the American Revolution (1775–83). The book was a runner-up for the prestigious Newbery Medal in 1975. It was also nominated for the American Book Award, and it won the James Addams Peace Prize. *With Every Drop of Blood,* published in 1994, was the Colliers' ninth book together. James Lincoln Collier has two children and lives in Pawling, New York. Christopher Collier has three children and lives in Orange, Connecticut.

Historical background of *With Every Drop of Blood*

The events in *With Every Drop of Blood* take place in Virginia during the final months of the Civil War. This was a conflict between the Northern part of the United States, known as the Union, and the Southern half of the country, known as the Confederacy. For many years before the war began in 1861, the two sides argued bitterly over several issues, including slavery.

Many people in the North believed that slavery was wrong and wanted to outlaw the practice. But the South's economy depended on slavery, and white Southerners argued that the national government should not interfere with their traditional way of life. When it became clear that the two sides could not reach an agreement, several Southern states seceded (withdrew) from the United States and formed their own country that allowed slavery, called the Confederate States of America, or the Confederacy. But Northern political leaders were determined not to let the Southern states leave the Union without a fight.

Johnny, the main character in *With Every Drop of Blood,* lives in Virginia's Shenandoah Valley. This was a very important region throughout the Civil War. The valley extends southwest from the Maryland border, in between the Blue Ridge and the Appalachian mountain chains. The northern end of the valley meets the Potomac River, which runs eastward into Washington, D.C. Since it provided easy access to the capital and other major Northern cities, the Confederates viewed the Shenandoah Valley as a natural route to use for an invasion of the North.

The valley was the sight of some impressive Southern victories in the early years of the war. In October 1861, the

Confederates placed Thomas "Stonewall" Jackson (1824–1863) in command of the Shenandoah Valley region. Jackson launched a brilliant military campaign the following spring. Although he had only seventeen thousand men, Jackson routinely defeated much larger Union forces in battle. He moved quickly and kept his opponents guessing about his location. It sometimes seemed as if Jackson's forces simply disappeared into the woods and mountains. At one point, President Abraham Lincoln (1809–1865) became convinced that Jackson was leading a major invasion of the North. The president ordered additional troops to return to Washington and protect the capital. Jackson's dazzling Shenandoah campaign baffled and frustrated Union leaders for months. It also kept eighty thousand Union troops busy and prevented them from joining the armies that were fighting in eastern Virginia at that time.

The fertile farmlands of the Shenandoah Valley also produced a great deal of meat and grain to feed the Confederate troops. In the later years of the war, the Shenandoah

Troops move through the Shenandoah Valley in September 1864. *Illustration by Alfred R. Waud. Courtesy of the Library of Congress.*

Union major general Philip H. Sheridan.
Courtesy of the National Archives and Records Administration.

became the main source of food for the Confederate forces under Robert E. Lee (1807–1870) that were defending the capital in Richmond. It also provided Southern armies with a place to hide. In 1864, for example, fifteen thousand Confederate cavalry troops under General Jubal Early (1816–1894) retreated into the valley. Union forces spent the entire summer trying to find them.

Union leaders eventually realized that they would never be able to capture Richmond as long as the Confederate army had access to the Shenandoah Valley. In the fall of 1864, the commander of all Union troops, General Ulysses S. Grant (1822–1885), decided that the answer was to destroy the valley. He sent General Philip Sheridan (1831–1888) into the Shenandoah region with forty thousand men. Their mission was to drive Early out of the valley and to eliminate the region as a source of supplies for Confederate forces. "Grant's instructions were grimly specific," Bruce Catton wrote in *The Civil War*. "He wanted the rich farmlands of the Valley despoiled [ruined] so thoroughly that the place could no longer support a Confederate army; he told Sheridan to devastate the whole area so thoroughly that a crow flying across over the Valley would have to carry its own rations."

The strategy Grant used in the Shenandoah Valley was known as "total warfare." This type of warfare involved not only the armies that were the official participants but also civilians (people not involved in the military, including women and children) and their property. Union leaders eventually came to believe that it was not enough to defeat Confederate forces on the field of battle. They felt that it was also necessary to break the spirit of the civilian population that supplied the army and supported the war effort.

Sheridan found the Confederate troops under Jubal Early in September and defeated them in a series of battles. Early then retreated down the valley, and Sheridan's forces began their grim work of destroying the region. "Few campaigns in the war aroused more bitterness than this one," Catton noted. "Barns and corncribs and gristmills and herds of cattle were military objectives now, and if thousands of civilians whose property this was had to suffer heartbreaking loss as a result, that was incidental [not important]. A garden spot was to be turned into a desert in order that the Southern nation might be destroyed." Although Sheridan's forces came under frequent attack from Confederate cavalry led by John Singleton Mosby (1833–1916)—a group known as Mosby's Rangers—the raids were not enough to stop the Union's campaign.

In *With Every Drop of Blood,* Union cavalry come to Johnny's farm in the Shenandoah Valley and steal his family's cow. The novel also mentions the Battle of Cedar Creek, where Johnny's father is wounded. This battle took place in October 1864. At this time, Sheridan thought he had taken control of the valley. He made a brief visit to Washington in order to give Union leaders a report on the progress of his campaign. On October 19, Confederate troops under General Early launched a surprise attack on Sheridan's camp near Cedar Creek. Some of the Union forces retreated, but Sheridan ran into the men on his way back from Washington. He turned them around and launched a counterattack. Early's forces suffered huge losses and were no longer a threat to the North.

Sheridan's destruction of the Shenandoah Valley made things very difficult for Lee's army to continue

Colonel John Singleton Mosby, leader of the Confederate cavalry unit called Mosby's Rangers.
Reproduced by permission of the Corbis Corporation.

In *With Every Drop of Blood,* the main character rides in a wagon train to help deliver food and supplies to Confederate troops. Here, a similar wagon delivers ammunition to troops. *Courtesy of the Library of Congress.*

guarding Richmond. Unable to get food or other supplies, Lee's forces grew ragged and hungry. In the novel, Johnny joins a wagon train that attempts to bring food to the desperate Confederate troops in Richmond. A group of Mosby's Rangers ride along to protect the supplies. Johnny ends up witnessing some of the final battles of the war in the area around the Confederate capital. The war finally ended in April 1865, when Lee surrendered to Grant at Appomattox Court House, Virginia.

Plot and characters of *With Every Drop of Blood*

The story in *With Every Drop of Blood* is told by Johnny, a fourteen-year-old farm boy from the Shenandoah Valley in Virginia. When the novel begins, Johnny's father has been away for several years fighting for the Confederate side in the Civil War. Johnny has become the man of the family in his father's absence. He works hard chopping firewood, plowing the fields, and helping his mother take care of his younger brother and sister. He also takes work as a teamster—carrying supplies for other people using his wagon and mules—to bring in extra money for the family.

Besides taking his father away, the war makes Johnny's life more difficult in other ways. "The Shenandoah Valley was about as hard hit as any place during the war," he explains. "The soil in the valley was rich and the crops always good—the barns busting out with corn, wheat, and hay, the cattle and hogs sleek and fat. The Southern army needed an awful lot of food every day and counted on the Shenandoah Valley to produce a good deal of it. Naturally, that brought on the Yankees. For months General Sheridan's bluecoats had been ranging up and down the valley, taking what they could carry off and destroying the rest—slaughtering our cattle and sheep, burning down our mills and whole barns full of corn and hay. It was awful. A crow would have to carry his own dinner if he was to fly across the Shenandoah Valley then." Union soldiers show up at Johnny's house one day and steal his cow while his family watches helplessly from their hiding spot in the woods.

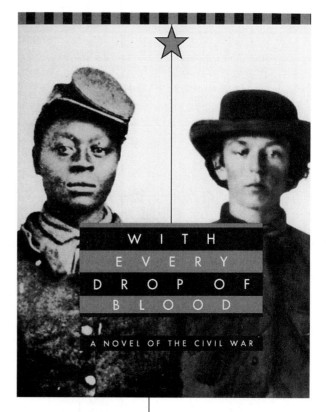

Cover of *With Every Drop of Blood*. *Designed by Jennifer Ann Daddio. Reproduced by permission of Dell Publishing Co.*

In the fall of 1864, Johnny's father finally returns home. He has been seriously wounded in the fighting at nearby Cedar Creek. But he finds the strength to share his views of the war with Johnny and teach him some of the things he needs to know to be the man of the family. Johnny's father thinks that the South is about to lose the war. He says that the Confederates cannot compete because the North has all the factories to produce weapons, ammunition, and clothing. The Union also has most of the ships and has been able to blockade Confederate ports and prevent food and other supplies from coming into the South.

Johnny's father explains that he joined the Confederate army because of states' rights—the idea that the state of Virginia had a right to govern itself without interference from the federal government. He says that the Southern states were forced to leave the Union because the Northern states had become too powerful. "The way it used to be, things were even between the North and the South," he says. "But things have changed. Now the North has the most states and the most people and has got rich from all those factories and such. They can outvote us in Congress whenever they want. If you give 'em the chance, they'll run the whole country to suit themselves." Johnny's father claims that his reasons for fighting had nothing to do with slavery. He says that the only people who were willing to fight to preserve slavery were a few rich plantation owners. "Why would I fight for slavery?" he asks. "We don't have slaves, nor do half the people in the valley, neither."

A few months after he returns home, Johnny's father gets an infection in his wound. He becomes very weak and realizes that he is dying. Before he dies, he makes Johnny promise not to go off and join the fighting. He says that he has already taken care of their duty to Virginia. He insists that his son stay at home and take care of the family. Johnny really wants to get revenge for his father's death, but he reluctantly agrees to honor his father's wishes. A short time later, Johnny takes his mules and wagon into a nearby town for supplies. While there, he runs into a friend of the family named Jeb Wagner. Jeb tells Johnny that a group of teamsters are putting together a wagon train to take food and supplies into Richmond, the capital of the Confederacy. At that time, Confederate forces under General Robert E. Lee were trying to defend the city against Union forces under General Ulysses S. Grant.

Johnny is very interested in joining the wagon train. He knows that the mission will be dangerous, but he also thinks it will be exciting. He likes the idea of bringing supplies to General Lee's army and helping the Confederate cause. He views it as a way to get back at the Yankees without actually doing any fighting. This way, he can technically keep his promise to his father. Johnny goes home and talks his mother into letting him join the wagon train. He assures her that he will be safe because a group of Mosby's Rangers will be going along to protect the wagon train. He also tells her that he will be able to earn some much-needed money to help support the family, and assures her that he will only be gone for a couple of weeks.

Civil War poster urging blacks to join the Union Army. *Public domain.*

When he sets out with the wagon train, Johnny has never been farther from home than the closest town. At first, the journey is very exciting for him and he enjoys looking around at the unfamiliar scenery. Before long, however, he begins seeing damage from the war—"houses with the windows and doors blown out of them; barns burnt to the ground; whole groves of trees broken and splintered where cannon balls had smashed through them, leaving tall stumps sticking up like bayonets. Once we passed a scattering of dead horses lying on a distant hillside, rotting and bloated."

Suddenly, the wagon train comes under attack by Union forces. The Mosby guards fight back, and there is shooting all around. Frightened by the attack, Johnny regrets his decision to join the wagon train. "I'd promised Pa I wouldn't go off to fight, and then I'd lied to Ma about there being no risk, and here I was in the middle of a fight after all. I felt awful, for there was a real chance now I'd get killed, or captured, and lose the mules and wagon in the bargain," he thinks. "What a blame fool I was." Johnny decides to try to hide from the enemy troops. He pulls his wagon and mules off the road and heads for some nearby woods. Just before he reaches safety, he is captured by a Union soldier.

Johnny is shocked when he sees that the soldier who has captured him is a black boy about his own age. Even though his family is too poor to own slaves, Johnny has been raised to believe that black people are inferior to whites. Like many other white people in the region where he lives, he often refers to blacks in negative, insulting terms. It does not make sense to him that this black boy is wearing a uniform, carrying a rifle, and telling him what to do. "It was a shock, all right— the world turned upside down," he says. "Oh, I'd heard that the Union army was taking blacks in. There'd been plenty about it in the newspapers, saying how it was an insult to our troops to have to fight against niggers—it was beneath the dignity of a white man. . . . Taking orders from a darky was another shock, especially one my own age. It was just the strangest thing, for I'd never heard a darky even speak back to a white person, much less give them orders."

When they return to the road, Johnny learns that the Union troops killed or chased off most of the Mosby guards and took control of the wagon train. Jeb Wagner, who was wounded in the fighting, is loaded into the back of Johnny's wagon. The soldier who captured Johnny, an escaped slave whose name is Cush Turner, rides on the seat of the wagon while Johnny rides on the back of one of his mules. Cush tells Johnny that they are taking the prisoners to City Point, a town that serves as a headquarters for Union troops in the area. From there, he says Johnny will be shipped to a prison camp in the North. Johnny is very upset at the idea of going to a prison camp. As they go toward City Point, he tries to think of a way to escape and return home to his family.

To comfort himself, Johnny starts reading passages of the Bible out loud. Cush is surprised to see that Johnny can read. Cush has always wanted to learn to read. Once, while he was a slave, he hid beneath the floor of a white school in order to learn the alphabet. But he was found and punished before he learned any more. Cush asks Johnny to teach him to read. In exchange, Cush offers to share his food and allow Johnny to sleep in a warm hayloft rather than in his wagon. But

Johnny resists the idea of teaching Cush to read. He knows that it is illegal in many parts of the South to educate black people. He also cannot understand why black people would need to be able to read, since most of them work in the fields their whole lives. Most of all, though, Johnny is angry with Cush for capturing him and acting like they are equal.

At first, Johnny tries to avoid teaching Cush to read by stalling. He asks Cush lots of questions about his life in order to keep him talking and make him forget about reading. In the process, Johnny learns a great deal about the cruel reality of slavery. He hears about how Cush's father was sold away from his family. He also learns that Cush was often whipped until he bled for small offenses, like eating a piece of ham from a pig that he had raised and butchered. Cush describes his escape from slavery, when his master sent dogs after him. He also talks about joining the Union army in order to help free his parents from slavery.

Confederate prisoners sit in a Union camp in the Shenandoah Valley in 1862.
Courtesy of the National Archives and Records Administration.

Hearing Cush's stories makes Johnny reconsider some of his ideas about slavery. He had always heard that black people were better off as slaves because they were not capable of caring for themselves. But talking to Cush makes him realize that some masters were mean to their slaves and that black people were unhappy under slavery. He can also understand Cush's desire to join the army to help free his parents. After all, the main reason Johnny wanted to join the wagon train was to honor his father.

After a while, Johnny cannot stall any longer. He decides that teaching Cush to read will be a good way to get friendly with him. This will cause Cush to let down his guard, which might give Johnny a chance to escape. Johnny is surprised when Cush wants to use a copy of President Abraham Lincoln's Gettysburg Address (see box in "John Burns of Gettysburg" entry) to learn to read. Cush keeps an old newspaper copy of the speech carefully preserved in his pocket. When Johnny sees how Cush values the speech, he must rethink more of his ideas about black people. "That little scrap of paper meant a whole lot to him," Johnny admits. "Abraham Lincoln was like Jesus Christ to him, and that piece of paper was holy, like a Bible or a gold cross was to some people. If I crunched it up, I didn't doubt but what he'd try to stick me for it. The whole thing brought me up short. Could a darky have holy feelings about things?"

But Johnny still resists the idea of teaching Cush to read. He is not sure that he should tell a black boy that the president said, "All men are created equal." So Johnny decides to teach Cush incorrectly. He mixes up similar words and sounds so that Cush will think he is learning to read, but will not understand the true meaning of the speech. For example, Johnny tells Cush that the speech says "all men are created *eagles.*"

As the wagon train continues moving toward City Point, Johnny keeps trying to find a way to escape. He almost succeeds when Jeb dies and he tells the Union soldiers that he is going to find a place to bury his body, but he gets caught at the last minute. At the same time, Johnny and Cush grow closer to one another. But Johnny still resists becoming friends with Cush because he is black. "To tell the truth, I wouldn't have minded having a friend right then," he says. "When you got down to it, he was a nice enough fella, willing to talk about things. And if he'd been white and on our side, I'd have jumped at the chance to make friends with him. To be honest, I'd have jumped at it even if he wasn't on our side. But I just couldn't bring myself to do that with a darky. Oh, I didn't mind being *friendly* with Cush, and rambling on about things; but that wasn't the same as being real friends."

The wagon train finally reaches City Point and pulls into the headquarters of Cush's unit. The white captain wants to ship Johnny off to a prison camp in the North, but Cush talks him out of it. He claims that Johnny is the only one who can control his mules. He tells the captain that they need to keep Johnny around long enough for Cush to learn to use his team and wagon. Johnny is surprised and grateful to Cush. He begins to feel badly about teaching Cush to read wrong.

The next day, the two boys go off on a wagon train mission to bring supplies to the Union troops along the front lines of battle near Petersburg. Along the way, Johnny learns that hundreds of Confederate soldiers have been surrendering every day because there is no food in the surrounded city. He also sees Confederate soldiers digging mass graves for their dead comrades.

Cush is injured when the wagon train comes under Confederate artillery fire. Johnny thinks about leaving Cush behind, but he feels that he owes Cush for saving him from the prison camp. He does not want Cush to get killed by a shell, captured by the Confederates, or punished by his captain for letting his prisoner escape. So Johnny puts Cush in the wagon and makes a break for it. They decide to head for the Shenandoah Valley, where Johnny lives and where Cush last saw his mother. They have to travel by night, because they could run into trouble from either side. Their journey goes well until Cush learns that Johnny was teaching him to read wrong. Cush becomes very angry and feels he cannot trust Johnny anymore. "You done it on purpose," Cush says, "for you was determined to keep me from finding out the real meaning of it—about all men being created equal—about what Lincoln promised, what the Declaration [of Independence, which Lincoln refers to in his speech] promised."

Cush runs away. Johnny goes after him, but they are soon caught by a group of Confederate cavalry. The riders leave Johnny and his wagon alone, but they take Cush prisoner. They plan to take him to the nearby town of Appomattox and shoot him as a Union spy. Johnny follows the riders to a tobacco barn outside of town. He tries to get Cush out of custody by telling the guards that Cush is his slave, but they refuse to release him. Johnny goes back to town to look for help. While there, he learns that Union general Ulysses S. Grant and Confederate general Robert E. Lee are about to meet to discuss terms of surrender. Johnny goes back to the barn and convinces the Confederate soldiers holding Cush that the war is over, and they release him.

The two boys decide to ride back toward home together. Johnny suggests that their journey might be easier if he rides in the wagon and Cush rides on one of the mules. He says that white people in the South would be used to seeing a white boy and a black boy traveling together that way. Cush does not like the idea. He argues that the whole reason for the Civil War was to give black people equal rights in American society. But Cush eventually agrees to ride on the mule. Both boys recognize that people's attitudes will not change immediately. But their own unlikely friendship gives them hope that things will improve over time. "For sure it is going to be a long time before kids of slaves and kids of slave owners will be able to sit together at the table of brotherhood, like the Bible says," Johnny thinks to himself. "But it was mighty hard for me to believe that Cush was lower than me. Could we still be friends? I didn't know. But I figured I'd try."

Style and themes in *With Every Drop of Blood*

James Lincoln Collier and Christopher Collier wrote *With Every Drop of Blood* in a first-person style. "First person" means that the narrator, or person who tells the story, is also a character in the story. The main character, Johnny, tells the story in *With Every Drop of Blood*. The authors probably chose this style because it would enable them to show readers Johnny's innermost thoughts. Readers can see what Johnny is feeling at different times. In this way, they can understand how his long-held beliefs and attitudes about black people change as his friendship with Cush develops.

The change in Johnny's feelings about black people and slavery is a major theme of the novel. As the story begins,

Johnny believes that black people are inferior to whites. His family is too poor to own slaves, and Johnny has not really known many black people. But he accepts what his parents and other Southerners have told him. Johnny's ideas about black people are based on stereotypes (generalized or overly simplified views of a group of people) rather than on his own experiences. When Johnny gets to know Cush, he is forced to question his views about black people. When Johnny hears Cush's stories about being a slave, he must rethink his ideas about slavery. Over the course of the story, Johnny gradually comes to believe that Cush is his equal and slavery is wrong. By the end of the book, Johnny is willing to risk his life to save his friend.

Another theme in *With Every Drop of Blood* centers around the idea that people in the South fought in the Civil War for many different reasons. Everyone that Johnny talks to about the war—from his father, to the other teamsters in the wagon train, to the Confederate soldiers he meets—has his own, different ideas about the reasons behind it. For example, Johnny's father tells him that the war is to protect states' rights. But Jeb Wagner tells him that it is to keep black people in slavery. Johnny struggles to make sense of the war and all the different reasons people have for fighting. He says at one point that "it seemed like a lot of people were fighting the Yanks just because they were here." After witnessing the horrors of war for himself, Johnny begins to wonder whether the whole conflict is pointless. It seems even more pointless to him once it ends, when he and Cush realize that racism still exists in the South. The boys understand that it will take much more than a lost war to change the attitudes of white people toward black people.

Research and Activity Ideas

1) Before Johnny meets Cush, he holds prejudiced views toward black people. Make a list of some of Johnny's wrong ideas about blacks and slavery. Why does he feel the way he does? As the story progresses and the two boys get to know one another, Johnny's attitudes change. Refer to your earlier list and give examples of how Johnny's relationship with Cush makes him rethink each of his prejudiced views.

2) Tell the class about an experience that made you rethink your attitudes or opinions, the way getting to know Cush made Johnny rethink his ideas about black people.

3) President Abraham Lincoln's Gettysburg Address is one of the most famous speeches in American history. Refer to the text of the speech elsewhere in this book. Why do you think Lincoln's words meant so much to Cush? Now replace the correct words in the Gettysburg Address with the incorrect words that Johnny teaches Cush. What was Johnny trying to accomplish by changing Lincoln's speech?

Related Titles

Burchard, Peter. *Jed, the Story of a Yankee Soldier and a Southern Boy.* New York: Coward-McCann, 1960. *In this novel, a sixteen-year-old Union soldier makes friends with an injured young Confederate supporter following the Battle of Shiloh.*

Donahue, John. *Island Far from Home.* Minneapolis: Carolrhoda Books, 1995. *This novel follows the relationship between a twelve-year-old Northern boy whose father is killed in the Civil War and a young Confederate prisoner of war.*

Polacco, Patricia. *Pink and Say.* New York: Philomel Books, 1994. *In this book for younger readers, Say Curtis meets a black soldier named Pinkus Aylee during the Civil War, and they are captured by Confederate troops.*

Reeder, Carolyn. *Across the Lines.* New York: Atheneum Books for Young Readers, 1997. *A novel that tells the parallel stories of twelve-year-old Edward, whose family must leave its plantation in the South during the Civil War, and his slave Simon, who escapes and joins the Union Army.*

Where to Learn More About . . .

The Colliers and *With Every Drop of Blood*

Brother Sam and All That: Historical Context and Literary Analysis of the Novels of James and Christopher Collier. Orange, CT: Clearwater Press, 1999.

"Collier, James Lincoln." *Educational Paperback Association.* [Online] http://www.edupaperback.org/authorbios/Collier_JamesLincoln.html (accessed on August 21, 2001).

Fifth Book of Junior Authors and Illustrators. New York: Wilson, 1983.

McElmeel, Sharron L. *The 100 Most Popular Children's Authors.* Libraries Unlimited, 1999.

Something about the Author. Vol. 70. Detroit: Gale, 1993.

"With Every Drop of Blood, By James Lincoln Collier and Christopher Collier." *Children's Literature Association of Utah.* [Online] http://www.slc.k12.ut.us/clau/clau9wed.htm (accessed on August 21, 2001).

The Shenandoah Valley Campaigns in the Civil War

Alexander, Bevin. *Lost Victories: The Military Genius of Stonewall Jackson.* New York: Holt, 1992.

Carter, Samuel. *The Last Cavaliers: Confederate and Union Cavalry in the Civil War.* New York: St. Martin's Press, 1980.

Catton, Bruce. *The Civil War.* Boston: Houghton Mifflin, 1960.

Farwell, Bryon. *Stonewall: A Biography of General Thomas J. Jackson.* Norton, 1992.

Heatwole, John L. *The Burning: Sheridan in the Shenandoah Valley.* Charlottesville, VA: Rockbridge, 1998.

Morris, Roy, Jr. *Sheridan: The Life and Wars of General Phil Sheridan.* New York: Crown, 1992.

Robertson, James I. Jr. *Stonewall Jackson: The Man, the Soldier, the Legend.* Macmillan, 1997.

American Civil War
Nonfiction Books

Perhaps no event in American history has been written about as much as the American Civil War (1861–65). During the Civil War era, countless Americans in both the North and the South discussed their wartime experiences and feelings in letters, journals, diaries, and memoirs. Ordinary soldiers wrote about their army friends, their frightening experiences in battle, and their dreams for a peaceful future. Famous generals, meanwhile, wrote about military strategy and battlefield tactics. In addition, thousands of mothers and wives from New England to the Deep South wrote about the challenges of providing for their families in wartime. They also wrote about their feelings after being reunited with long-absent husbands or burying beloved sons. Finally, leading writers and journalists of both regions published essays and reports on a wide range of war-related subjects, from major battles to slavery.

The Civil War ended in 1865 after four years of terrible bloodshed. Americans continued to write about the conflict long after the soldiers had laid down their rifles and returned home. After all, the war had ended slavery across the nation, and it had forever changed the lives of millions of Americans, both black and white. Ordinary men and women continued to record their personal memories of the war in journals and diaries. Historians attempted to explain the war and its major battles in hundreds of books and articles.

This effort to explain the causes, events, and impacts of the Civil War continues nearly a century and a half after the conflict's final shots were fired. Modern historians publish all kinds of books about the war for readers of all ages. Some of these works provide an overview of the entire conflict. Thousands of other nonfiction books, however, focus on one single aspect of the Civil War. For example, James McPherson's book *For Cause and Comrades* examines the emotions and motives of Civil War soldiers. In *Gettysburg: The Final Fury,* author Bruce Catton covers the great Battle of Gettysburg that took place in Pennsylvania in 1863. Historian Stephen B. Oates's book *With Malice Toward None* is a biography of President Abraham Lincoln, whereas Samuel Carter's book *The Last Cavaliers* is devoted to the Confederate and Union cavalries of the Civil War. Hundreds of other nonfiction Civil War books have been published as well. These include biographies of military and political leaders, studies of battles and military tactics, and books that explain the wartime feelings and experiences of slaveowners, abolitionists, women, African Americans, children, Southerners, Northerners, and many other groups.

Four nonfiction works are featured in *Experiencing the American Civil War.* Each work covers a different subject area of the Civil War. Jim Murphy's book *The Boys' War: Confederate and Union Soldiers Talk about the Civil War* describes the wartime experiences of the thousands of teenage boys who fought in the Union or Confederate armies during the conflict. The author combines diary entries and letters written by these boys with photographs from the Civil War era to document the experiences and emotions of these young, brave soldiers.

North Star to Freedom by Gena Kinton Gorrell tells the story of the Underground Railroad, a secret network of homes, shops, and barns scattered across the American South where escaped slaves received food and shelter on their dangerous journey to freedom in the northern United States and Canada. It also discusses the history of slavery in North America and explains the long fight to abolish the practice in America's Southern states.

Mary Chesnut's Civil War is the Civil War diary of a wealthy white Southern woman. Today, Chesnut's diary is the most famous of all the personal journals written during the Civil War era. Full of entertaining comments on the South's leading politicians, generals, and plantation owners, it also contains strikingly honest remarks on slavery, war, and the traditions of Southern society.

Zak Mettger's book *Till Victory Is Won: Black Soldiers in the Civil War* relates the experiences of black Union soldiers during the Civil War. It also explains how the soldiers' brave performance during the conflict became a stepping stone to freedom for all black Americans.

Representative Nonfiction Books about the Civil War

Benson, Berry. *Berry Benson's Civil War Book: Memoirs of a Confederate Scout and Sharpshooter*. Athens: University of Georgia Press, 1962, 1992. *Thousands of Civil War journals and memoirs written by ordinary soldiers have been published over the years, but few are as interesting as this book by Benson, who scouted for Confederate general Robert E. Lee during the war.*

Carter, Samuel. *The Last Cavaliers*. New York: St. Martin's Press, 1979. *Carter's book is devoted to the Confederate and Union cavalries of the Civil War.*

Catton, Bruce. *Gettysburg: The Final Fury*. Garden City, NY: Doubleday, 1974. *This book covers the great battle of Gettysburg that took place in Pennsylvania in 1863.*

Chesnut, Mary Boykin. *Mary Chesnut's Civil War*. Edited by C. Vann Woodward. New Haven, CT: Yale University Press, 1981. *This book is the Civil War diary of a wealthy white Southern woman. Today, Chesnut's diary is the most famous of all the personal journals written during the Civil War era.*

Freedman, Russell. *Lincoln: A Photobiography*. New York: Clarion Books, 1987. *This Newbery Medal–winner uses text and photographs to tell the story of President Abraham Lincoln, who guided the North to victory in the Civil War, restoring the Union in the process.*

Gorrell, Gena Kinton. *North Star to Freedom*. New York: Delacorte Press, 1997. *Gorrell tells the story of the Underground Railroad, a secret network of places where escaped slaves received food and shelter on their dangerous journey to freedom in the northern United States and Canada.*

Grant, Ulysses S. *Personal Memoirs of U. S. Grant*. New York: C. L. Webster, 1885. Multiple subsequent editions. *This autobiographical account by Union general U. S. Grant, who also served as president of the United States from 1869 to 1877, ranks as one of the greatest memoirs in American literature.*

Leonard, Elizabeth. *All the Daring of the Soldier: Women of the Civil War Armies*. New York: W. W. Norton, 1999. *This work explains the many ways in which women contributed to the war effort in both the North and the South.*

Marrin, Albert. *Unconditional Surrender: U. S. Grant and the Civil War* and *Virginia's General: Robert E. Lee and the Civil War*. New York: Maxwell Macmillan International, 1994. *These two works follow the lives of the Civil War's most famous generals, Union commander Ulysses S. Grant and Confederate legend Robert E. Lee.*

McPherson, James. *For Cause and Comrades*. New York: Oxford University Press, 1997. *This book examines the emotions and motives of Civil War soldiers.*

Meltzer, Milton. *Voices from the Civil War*. New York: Crowell, 1989. *This book uses letters, diary entries, and other personal recollections to showcase the feelings of Northern and Southern communities, black and white people, and male and female Americans when the Civil War shook the nation.*

Mettger, Zak. *Till Victory Is Won: Black Soldiers in the Civil War*. New York: Lodestar Books, 1994. *Mettger's book relates the experiences of black Union soldiers during the Civil War.*

Mitchell, Reid. *The Vacant Chair: The Northern Soldier Leaves Home*. New York: Oxford University Press, 1993. *A nonfiction book that describes how Northern homes and communities coped when husbands and sons left home to fight in the Civil War.*

Murphy, Jim. *The Boys' War: Confederate and Union Soldiers Talk about the Civil War*. New York: Clarion Books, 1990. *Murphy's book describes the wartime experiences of the thousands of teenage boys who fought in the Union or Confederate armies during the conflict.*

Oates, Stephen B. *With Malice Toward None*. New York: Harper & Row, 1977. *Oates' book is a biography of President Abraham Lincoln.*

Smith, John D. *Black Voices from Reconstruction*. Brookfield, CT: Millbrook Press, 1996. *This book relates the post–Civil War experiences of dozens of former slaves.*

Trudeau, Noah. *Like Men of War: Black Troops in the Civil War, 1862–1865*. Boston: Little, Brown, 1998. *This work focuses on the experiences of black Union soldiers, highlighting the performances of famous black regiments like the 54th Massachusetts.*

Wiley, Bell Irvin. *The Life of Johnny Reb*. Indianapolis: Bobbs-Merrill, 1943. Reprint, Baton Rouge: Louisiana State University Press, 1978. *The Life of Billy Yank*. Indianapolis: Bobbs-Merrill, 1952. Reprint, Baton Rouge: Louisiana State University Press, 1978. *These books describe the experiences of Confederate and Union soldiers in camp, on the march, and on the battlefield.*

The Boys' War

Written by Jim Murphy

Thousands of the soldiers who fought in the American Civil War (1861–65) were actually boys who were under the age of eighteen. Jim Murphy's nonfiction book *The Boys' War: Confederate and Union Soldiers Talk about the Civil War* tells the story of these boys, who were only in their mid-teens when they found themselves fighting for their lives on the battlefields of Virginia, Tennessee, and Pennsylvania. Murphy uses diary entries and letters written by these boys, as well as numerous photographs from the Civil War era, to create a work that documents the experiences and emotions of these young, brave soldiers.

Biography of author Jim Murphy

Jim Murphy was born on September 25, 1947, in Newark, New Jersey. He is the son of James K. Murphy, an accountant, and Helen Irene Grosso Murphy, a bookkeeper and artist. Murphy grew up in Kearny, New Jersey, in a neighborhood of Scottish, Irish, and Italian families. "My friends and I did all the normal things—played baseball and football endlessly, explored abandoned factories, walked the railroad tracks

Jim Murphy, author of *The Boys' War.* *Reproduced by permission of Houghton Mifflin Company.*

to the vast Jersey Meadowlands, and, in general, cooked up as much mischief as we could," he recalled in *Contemporary Authors.* "And since Kearny was close to both Newark and New York City, we would often hop a bus or train to these cities. We loved wandering through those places—so much different than our comfortable, tree-lined streets— watching the people and eating strange and usually greasy foods."

Murphy admits that he was not much of a reader as a youngster. In high school, however, a teacher proclaimed that none of his students should ever read *A Farewell to Arms,* a book written by Ernest Hemingway (1899–1961). The teacher's warning intrigued Murphy, who promptly found a copy and read it from cover to cover. He enjoyed *A Farewell to Arms* so much that he started reading other books and even began writing his own short stories and poetry.

After graduating from high school, Murphy enrolled at Rutgers University in New Brunswick, New Jersey. He left Rutgers with a bachelor's degree in 1970. Later that year, he accepted a job at Seabury Press (later known as Clarion Books) as an editorial secretary. He moved up steadily through the editorial ranks of the publishing company, eventually achieving the position of managing editor. But in 1977, he decided to leave the firm and support himself as a freelance writer and editor. (Working freelance means that instead of working for just one publisher, a person sells his or her work to a number of companies.)

Since Murphy began his freelance career, he has written many books for children's and young adult audiences. At first, he concentrated on writing lighthearted or suspenseful novels for children. Over time, however, he became fond of writing nonfiction books about various eras in American history. These projects gave him an opportunity to satisfy his own natural curiosity about past historic events. One of his best known nonfiction history books is *The Great Fire* (1996), which tells readers about an 1871 fire that burned down much of the city of Chicago, Illinois. Another popular book written by Murphy is *Blizzard! The Storm that Changed America* (2000). In this work, the author recalls a terrible snowstorm that hit the northeastern United States in 1888, killing hundreds of people. The blizzard, which also caused great financial damage to the region, convinced the U.S. government to build up its national weather bureau so that American communities would have greater advance warning of future storms.

Murphy has also written several books about the American Civil War for young adult audiences over the years. In 1998, he wrote *The Journal of James Edmond Pease: A Civil War Union Soldier* as part of the *My Name Is America* children's book series. Two years later, he published a nonfiction book about the Battle of Gettysburg called *The Long Road to Gettysburg*.

Murphy's best-known book about the Civil War, though, is *The Boys' War: Confederate and Union Soldiers Talk about the Civil War*. In this work, published in 1990, Murphy examines the experiences of young Civil War soldiers. He uses the actual letters and diaries of boys who fought in the war to show their feelings about combat, homesickness, life in the army camps, and other aspects of the conflict. "It's true that their writing lacks a historian's ability to focus on the 'important issues,'" stated Murphy in *The Boys' War.* "But it is this directness and eye for everyday details that make the voices of these boys so fresh and believable and eloquent. And it is their ability to create active, vivid scenes that brings the war, in all its excitement and horror, alive after more than one hundred years."

Historical background of *The Boys' War*

No one knows for sure how many boys took up arms as soldiers in the American Civil War. According to Murphy, historians have estimated that as many as twenty percent of all soldiers in the Civil War (more than four hundred thousand total) were under the age of eighteen when they signed up. But incomplete records from that period make it impossible to determine the true percentage of underage troops.

Although the exact number of boy soldiers will forever be a mystery, letters, journals, newspaper articles, and oral his-

Males under the age of eighteen often lied about their age and joined the army or helped out a regiment in an unofficial way. Here, a young boy, known as a powder monkey, helps out on the Union warship *New Hampshire* by bringing ammunition to the gun crew. *Reproduced by permission of Archive Photos.*

tories from the Civil War period make it clear that thousands of adolescents participated in the war's military campaigns. In addition, this evidence made it possible for future generations to gain insights into the lives of these young soldiers. "We might not know how many boys took part in the war, but we certainly have a clear picture of what they experienced and felt," wrote Murphy. "Almost every soldier sent letters home, and a surprising number kept journals and diaries, wrote memoirs about their adventures or articles and histories of their companies."

Certainly most boys who lived in America during the Civil War never came near a battlefield. They spent their childhoods playing, going to school, doing chores, or even working to provide money for their families. But the war still changed their lives in dramatic ways. Many children had fathers or brothers who were killed or crippled in the war, and countless children in the Southern states saw their family's homes or farm fields destroyed by the war's violence.

Children also contributed to the war effort in many ways that did not involve military service. For example, schoolchildren were often recruited to scrape lint away from linens and garments; this lint was later used in hospitals to pack the wounds of injured soldiers. Children also sold flowers, fruit, or other items to raise money to purchase flags, medical supplies for military hospitals, or food for wounded soldiers who could not provide for themselves.

As the war progressed, its impact on America's children and young adults continued to grow. "Despite the vast differences in how northern and southern, as well as black and white, children experienced the war, they were united in their responses to the crisis," wrote James Marten in *The Children's Civil War.* "Magazines, novels, and schoolbooks offered children examples of how they could honorably and usefully support their country. From them they learned to identify good and evil, Yankee and Rebel, and the right and wrong ways to act. . . . If children's reading matter awakened young patriots, letters from their fathers, which also educated and directed children's actions, energized them. As children strove to match the expectations raised by stories and books and to perform the duties set forth by fathers, they became a part of the struggle, not just as victims or spectators but as politicians and home-front warriors."

The Drummer Boy of Chickamauga

Of all the youths who served during the Civil War as drummer boys, a boy named Johnny Clem ranks as the most famous of them all. Born in August 1851 in Newark, Ohio, he was not even ten years old when the war began in April 1861. But his young age did not stop Clem from running away from home in May to join the Union army.

Clem's initial efforts to join the military failed miserably. Union officers turned him down time and time again, telling him that he was too young even to be a drummer boy. But the youngster refused to give up. When the commander of Michigan's 22nd regiment told him to go home, Clem instead tagged along with the company. Many of the soldiers admired the young lad's bravery and persistence, and before long he became a sort of mascot to the regiment.

As Clem traveled with the regiment, he performed many of the duties of a drummer boy. He helped out with chores, fed the horses, and practiced his drumming with an old drum that some of the soldiers found for him. At first, he received no money for his work, because he was not an official member of the military. After several weeks, however, the commander of the regiment joined with other officers to take up a collection for Clem. They also agreed to donate a portion of their own salaries to the boy in future months. The generosity of the officers made it possible for the youngster to receive a regular soldier's pay.

In April 1862, the Twenty-second Michigan regiment took part in the Battle of Shiloh in Tennessee. During this bloody battle, which killed or wounded twenty-three thousand Union and Confederate soldiers, a flying fragment from a cannonball destroyed Clem's drum but left him unharmed. After the battle was over, the other soldiers began calling the boy "Johnny Shiloh" in recognition of both his bravery and luck on the battlefield. Newspapers picked up on the story, and soon people all across the North and the South knew of the war's littlest drummer boy.

Clem's legend grew in October 1863, at the Battle of Chickamauga. During that terrible fight— which produced a total of thirty-four thousand casualties on the two sides—Clem actually participated in the

Indeed, games based on the Civil War dominated backyards and playgrounds. Children acted out all aspects of the war, pretending that they were famous generals, soldiers, nurses, or prisoners. But many teenage boys felt a deep desire to actually participate in the war as soldiers. They saw the war as an opportunity for them to defend their homes, have a great adventure,

Johnny Clem, at nine years old, one of the youngest drummer boys when he "joined" the Union army a month after the Civil War started. *Reproduced by permission of Archive Photos.*

shouted at the boy to surrender. But instead, Clem silently raised his musket and shot the soldier off his horse. For this coolness under fire, the boy acquired a second nickname—"The Drummer Boy of Chickamauga"—and was named an honorary sergeant.

A few months later, General George H. Thomas (1816–1870) assigned Clem to his staff as a mounted courier. Clem remained a courier until the last few months of the war, when he was discharged from the Union army. After the war, Clem repeatedly tried to enroll at the West Point Military Academy, but his lack of schooling made it impossible for him to pass the entrance exam. Aided by President Ulysses S. Grant (1822–1885), Clem returned to the army in 1871 at the rank of second lieutenant. He spent the next forty-five years in the military, rising to the rank of major general. When he retired from the army in 1916, he became the last Civil War veteran to leave active army service. Clem died on May 13, 1937, in San Antonio, Texas. He was buried in Arlington National Cemetery, the national military cemetery located in Virginia, just outside of Washington, D.C.

fighting. Armed with a rifle trimmed to his size, he rode into battle on an artillery caisson (pronounced KAY-sahn; an ammunition box on wheels). As the fighting progressed, the Union forces fell into a panicked retreat. During the retreat, a Confederate soldier recognized Clem. Eager to capture the famous child, the rebel gave chase and

and graduate to manhood. "Some boys refused to settle for heckling raw recruits, maneuvering paper soldiers around bedroom floors, or shuffling through drills with broomstick rifles," wrote Marten. "Fascinated by the sudden militarization [preparation for war] of their society and aching for adventure, they became obsessed with the idea of joining the army."

Of course, many parents forbade their underage sons from joining the war. But some boys simply ran away from home in order to fulfill their dream. In a few cases, teenage boys who were prevented from joining the army became so upset that they made tragic decisions to take their own lives. In 1862, for example, a seventeen-year-old Ohio boy hanged himself when his parents would not allow him to join his older brothers in the Union army. Two years later, a thirteen-year-old boy who wanted to enlist with the Confederates killed himself with a gunshot wound to the head when his mother refused to let him go.

During the Civil War, both North and South instituted rules prohibiting boys under age eighteen from joining their armies. But these rules could easily be avoided by a teenage boy if he looked fairly mature and was willing to lie about his age. After all, noted Murphy, "How would a recruiter check on an applicant's facts? The standard forms of identification we have today, such as driver's license, social security number, and credit cards, did not exist back then. There were no computers or telephones, either, so verifying someone's birthday was nearly impossible."

In addition, some underage boys found that they could gain admittance into the army if they applied for drummer or bugler positions. Since these were viewed as "nonfighting" positions, recruiters did not worry about the age of the boys who filled those roles. Although their duties included cooking and carrying water, caring for horses, and other everyday camp chores, drummer boys were also an important factor in the success of military operations. "The beat of the drum was one of the most important means of communicating orders to soldiers in the Civil War," explained Murphy. "Drummers did find themselves in camp sounding the routine calls to muster [roll call] or meals and providing the beat for marching drills. But more often than not, they were with the troops in the field, not just marching to the site of the battle but in the middle of the fighting. It was the drumbeat that told the soldiers how and when to maneuver as smoke poured over the battlefield. And the sight of a drummer boy showed soldiers where their unit was located, helping to keep them close together. Drummers were such a vital part of battle communication that they often found themselves the target of enemy fire" (see box).

During the conflict, many underage soldiers performed well on the battlefield, showing bravery and skill even in the most chaotic and dangerous situations. After the Civil War concluded, however, the U.S. government took steps to make sure that boys would never serve in the military again. Military leaders, politicians, and parents alike agreed that war was no place for a fifteen- or sixteen-year-old boy to be. With this in mind, the government made it virtually impossible for boys under the age of eighteen to join the U.S. military, even as musicians, cooks, or telegraph operators.

Subject matter of _The Boys' War_

Murphy begins _The Boys' War_ by admitting that "for most of us, the Civil War is an event we meet briefly in our history books, a distant and sometimes dry parade of proclamations, politicians, generals, and battles. But for the soldiers who marched off and fought, the Civil War was all too real and consuming." He urges readers to recognize that military service during the Civil War was especially challenging for the tens of thousands of underage boys who fought in the conflict.

In the opening pages of his book, Murphy provides a brief overview of the political and social causes of the Civil War. For example, he notes that the great economic and cultural differences between the North and the South produced very different feelings about slavery. The North saw it as an evil practice, whereas the South saw it as essential to its economic survival. Murphy also points out that the South supported the concept of "states' rights," a belief that each state has the right to handle various issues for itself without interference from the national government. The North, on the other hand, believed that the federal government should be able to pass laws that all states should follow. "When war actually broke out . . . the country seemed to sigh with relief," wrote Murphy. "Something concrete was finally going to settle the dispute."

The first chapter of *The Boys' War* shows how boys in both the North and the South rushed to join the military in the opening weeks of the war. Hungry to show off their patriotism or experience a grand adventure, Northern and Southern boys alike lied to recruiters in order to gain admittance into the army. In the next chapter, Murphy uses excerpts from boys' letters and journals to provide readers with information on the early months of the war, when both sides concentrated on outfitting and training their new troops.

The book's third chapter focuses on the horrors of Civil War combat. It shows how the war's terrible violence—whether seen in a major battle or a small skirmish—made boy soldiers rethink their belief that war was a grand adventure. For example, a fifteen-year-old Union soldier named Elisha Stockwell (1846–1935) wrote after his first battle that "I want to say, as we lay there and the shells were screaming over us, my thoughts went back to my home, and I thought what a foolish boy I was to run away and get into such a mess as I was in. I would have been glad to have seen my father coming after me." In chapter four, Murphy turns his attention to the boy drummers who served both armies during the war.

The second half of Murphy's book explores the daily lives of young Civil War soldiers. He talks about the general living conditions of the army camps and explains how "camp life with all of its comforts and discomforts created a lasting bond between soldiers. In a real way, this shared experience made the others in each soldier's company both his family and his friends." The author also devotes a chapter to the ways in which constant exposure to the war's brutality made many young soldiers numb to the suffering and pain around them. For example, Murphy quotes a letter written by a young soldier named Henry Graves: "I saw the body of a man killed the previous day this morning and a horrible sight it was. Such sights do not effect me as they once did. I can not describe the change nor do I know when it took effect, yet I know that there is a change for I look on the carcass [body] of a man with pretty much such feeling as I would do were it a horse or dog."

In the closing chapters of *The Boys' War,* the author discusses the awful living conditions that existed in many Civil

War prison camps. He also tells readers about the common fear—shared by Yankee and Rebel soldiers alike—of dying alone in some forgotten corner of a battlefield, or of enduring amputation or other painful medical treatments in one of the war's bloody field hospitals.

Finally, *The Boys' War* covers the reaction of boy soldiers when the war finally ends in 1865 and their feelings upon returning home. Northerners returned to parades and happy celebrations, while Southerners rode home alone through areas that still bore the marks of the war. But soldiers on both sides shared the knowledge that their wartime experiences had changed them forever. For example, Murphy tells the story of one Southern boy who makes it back to his family's home after spending days avoiding Union soldiers and scrounging for food. "I reached home May 25th, 1865," the young soldier recalled. "I found my father and mother working in the garden. Neither knew me at first glance, but when I smiled and spoke to them, mother recognized me and with tears of joy clasped me to her arms. My father stood by gazing upon me in mute [silent] admiration. Their long-lost boy had been found."

Style and themes in *The Boys' War*

Murphy arranges *The Boys' War* in chronological order, providing coverage from the war's earliest days to its final hours. Throughout the book, the author uses historical materials to discuss the Civil War experiences of underage soldiers. He reprints excerpts of actual letters and journals written by fourteen-, fifteen-, and sixteen-year-old soldiers to show the conditions and challenges that these teenagers faced. He also includes many historical photographs from the Civil War era in his book. These pictures range from portraits of individual soldiers, drummer units, and army camps to grim battlefield photographs showing the lifeless bodies of fallen soldiers.

The Boys' War covers all major aspects of the Civil War, from the terror of battle to the routine of camp chores. As the book discusses these various subjects, it pays special attention to the experiences of underage soldiers. In fact, the book's major purpose is to show how these youngsters were changed by their wartime experiences. When these young soldiers first go off to war, they are scared, excited teenagers. But the ones who survive the war to return home to friends and family are forever changed. Their exposure to the realities of war—including the violent deaths of close friends—forces them to grow up in a hurry.

Research and Activity Ideas

1) *The Boys' War* uses letters and journals written by teenage soldiers to explain what military life was like for them during the Civil War. Indeed, many men and boys who participated in the war recorded their experiences through diaries and long letters. Today, however, relatively few people keep diaries or write long letters to friends or family. Why do you think that this practice has become less common? Do you think people are more likely to write down their thoughts and feelings in times of war?

2) Imagine that you must leave your family to join the U.S. Army. You fool the army into accepting you despite your young age, and you undergo training as a combat soldier. Pretend that you have just learned that you are being sent into battle tomorrow, and that you only have time to write one letter to your family before you leave. In your letter, tell them what you miss most about home and explain how you are feeling about your situation.

3) Write an imaginary account of an actual Civil War battle from the perspective of a young Confederate or Union drummer boy. The account can either be written as a diary entry, or it can be written in the form of a letter home to family.

Where to Learn More About . . .

Jim Murphy

Authors and Artists for Young Adults. Vol. 20. Detroit: Gale Research, 1997.

Contemporary Authors. Vol. 111. Detroit: Gale Research, 1984.

Boy Soldiers in the Civil War

Lord, Francis A., and Arthur Wise. *Bands and Drummer Boys of the Civil War.* New York: Yoseloff, 1966.

Marten, James. *The Children's Civil War.* Chapel Hill: University of North Carolina Press, 1998.

Mitchell, Reid. *Civil War Soldiers: Their Expectations and Their Experiences.* New York: Viking, 1988.

Mary Chesnut's Civil War

Written by Mary Boykin Chesnut

Mary Boykin Chesnut (1823–1886) is the most famous diarist of the American Civil War (1861–65). Her journal, published as *Mary Chesnut's Civil War* in 1981, is one of the most entertaining and historically important works produced by a member of the Confederacy. Historians value Chesnut's work for a number of reasons. For example, it provides a treasure of information on the lifestyles and attitudes of the rich white Southern plantation society of which she was a member. But the diary, which Chesnut faithfully kept throughout the conflict, also provides a fascinating reflection of the wartime hopes and fears of the entire South.

Biography of author Mary Boykin Chesnut

Mary Boykin Miller Chesnut was born in Statesburg, South Carolina, on March 31, 1823. She was the oldest child of Mary Boykin and Stephen Decatur Miller. Chesnut's father was a wealthy plantation owner who also had great political power. He served his home state as both a U.S. congressman and senator at various times, and he was elected governor of South Carolina when Chesnut was three years old.

Famous Civil War diarist Mary Boykin Chesnut (right) and her husband, U.S. senator James Chesnut of South Carolina.
Reproduced by permission of the Granger Collection Ltd.

Chesnut's parents made sure that she received the best education available. She attended exclusive private schools in Camden and Charleston, where she learned to speak French and German and developed a lifelong interest in literature. In April 1840, she married James Chesnut, the son of one of South Carolina's wealthiest landowners. After the wedding ceremony, the seventeen-year-old bride moved with her husband to Mulberry, the Chesnut family's huge cotton plantation outside of Camden. She spent the next eighteen years at the plantation, which used large numbers of slaves to work the cotton fields and take care of housekeeping duties around the mansion. During this time, her greatest source of unhappiness was her inability to have children and raise a family.

In 1858, James Chesnut was elected to the U.S. Senate. He and his wife moved to Washington, D.C., where they established friendships with many of the nation's political leaders. In early 1861, however, Chesnut's husband resigned his senate seat to protest the election of Abraham Lincoln (1809–1865) as president of the United States. Like many other Southerners, James Chesnut believed that the election of Lincoln—a politician from the North, which opposed slavery—meant that the federal government would soon try to abolish (put an end to) slavery in the South. This fear rippled all across the South, which depended on slaves to power its agriculture-based economy. Within weeks of Lincoln's election, eleven Southern slaveholding states declared that they were leaving the United States and forming their own nation, called the Confederate States of America, or the Confederacy. But Lincoln and the states that remained part of the United States refused to accept the division of the country. They vowed to keep the United States together as one nation. A short time later, the first shots of the American Civil War were fired.

Confederate president Jefferson Davis. *Courtesy of the Library of Congress.*

The Chesnuts left Washington in early 1861 and returned to South Carolina, where James became one of the Confederacy's early political leaders. During this time, Mary began keeping her famous diary, in part because she recognized that the war was a major historical event. "The scribbling mania is strong in me," she wrote in October 1861. "I have an insane idea in my brain to write a tale." In 1862, her husband was named an official aide to Confederate president Jefferson Davis (1808–1889), so they moved to Richmond, Virginia, the Confederate capital. Once the Chesnuts settled in Richmond, their home became a social gathering place for the Confederacy's most important couples, including President Davis and his wife Varina. Mary Chesnut hosted countless dinners and teas during this period, listening intently as her guests gossiped about their friends or discussed the war. She then described her impressions of these and other events in diary entries.

The Chesnuts spent the last months of the war moving from city to city, as Union forces pushed deeper into the Confederacy. After the Confederate army finally surrendered in April 1865, the Chesnuts returned home to South Carolina. But upon arriving, they discovered that their Mulberry plantation had been destroyed by the Union army.

Burdened with heavy financial debts, the Chesnuts struggled to rebuild their lives after the war. Mary, for example, resorted to selling eggs, milk, and other dairy products to put food on the table. At times, the struggle seemed almost too much for Mary Chesnut to bear. "There are nights here with the moonlight, cold & ghastly & the whippoorwills, & the screech owls alone disturbing the silence when I could tear my hair & cry aloud for all that is past & gone," she admitted in one letter.

But over time, the Chesnuts paid off their debts, and they moved to a smaller but comfortable home in Camden in 1873. Chesnut then returned her attention to the wartime diary she had kept. Eager to see it published, she rewrote many sections and deleted other portions that might embarrass her friends. (For example, she eliminated remarks about the poor table manners of President Davis and his wife.) She continued to work on her diary until 1885, when both her husband and her mother died. Mary Chesnut died one year later, on November 22, 1886, in Camden, South Carolina.

When Chesnut died, she left her personal papers to her friend Isabella Martin. In 1905, a version of Chesnut's Civil War diary, called *A Diary from Dixie,* was finally published. Another version of the diary was published in 1949. Like the first edition, however, it did not include many of Chesnut's most interesting remarks about her friends and experiences. But the 1981 edition of her diary, edited by historian C. Vann Woodward and published as *Mary Chesnut's Civil War,* restored these historically valuable and entertaining passages. This version of Chesnut's diary received the Pulitzer Prize for nonfiction and confirmed her place as one of the most important writers of the Civil War era. Today, *Mary Chesnut's Civil War*—full of gossip, witty remarks, and heartfelt commentary about slavery, Southern society, and the Civil War itself—continues to be hailed as perhaps the finest literary work to come out of the Confederacy.

Historical background of *Mary Chesnut's Civil War*

The Civil War changed the lives of American women forever. Before the war, women occupied an inferior place in communities in both the North and the South. They had few legal rights and found it almost impossible to escape American society's belief that a woman's place was in the home, where she was expected to spend her time doing domestic chores, caring for children, and obeying her husband or father.

But when the Civil War began, hundreds of thousands of men left their families and communities to join the Confederate or Union armies. As a result, women were left to assume many responsibilities that had traditionally been carried out by men. These new responsibilities included cutting firewood for cold winters, planting crops, earning money to feed and shelter children, and—in the case of some Southern women—supervising slaves. Women also stepped out of their traditional roles as homemakers by contributing to the war effort as nurses, aid workers, spies, factory employees, and government clerks. "Women stepped forward as defenders of their respective causes," stated Mary Elizabeth Massey in *Women in the Civil War*. "Emotions, energies, and talents that even they did not realize they possessed were unleashed. Here was a crusade in which they were needed and one in which they enthusiastically participated. . . . Women did not have to go to the front or serve in distant hospitals to support their cause; they encountered battles aplenty at home."

In many respects, the wartime challenges that confronted white women in the North and the South were the same. But two factors made the task of household leadership especially difficult for Southern women. First, most of the war was fought on Southern soil. As a result, many homes in the South were destroyed, and shortages of basic necessities such as food, clothing, and shelter became common across much of the region. These threats made it even more challenging for Southern women to provide for their families.

The second factor that made the Civil War especially difficult for Southern women was that they were even less prepared to assume family leadership roles than women of the North. Southern traditions defined white women as beautiful but delicate flowers who had to be protected from the rougher aspects of

THE INFLUENCE

OF WOMAN

THE SISTER OF CHARITY

HOME TIDINGS

Illustration entitled "The Influence of Woman," showing scenes of women aiding the war effort by sewing, washing, and writing letters for and praying with wounded soldiers. *From the September 6, 1862, issue of* Harper's Weekly. *Courtesy of the Library of Congress.*

life. These views were especially strong in the South's wealthy plantation households, like the one in which Mary Chesnut lived. So when white men left these plantations to fight for the Confederacy, they left behind mothers, wives, and daughters with little experience in taking care of themselves. "Socialized to believe in their own weakness and sheltered from the necessity of performing even life's basic tasks, many white women felt almost crippled by their unpreparedness for the new lives war had brought," stated Drew Gilpin Faust in *Mothers of Invention*.

Some women wilted under the wartime pressure of providing for themselves and their families. Others fought with all their energy to keep their families together until the war's conclusion, only to give up hope upon learning that their husbands, sons, or fathers had died in battle. As the war progressed, however, many women discovered—sometimes to their surprise—that they were capable of meeting wartime's challenges without the assistance of men. This realization gave some of them the confidence to question their traditional place in American society. "Through the experiences of war, white southern women [came] to a new understanding of themselves and their interests as women," said Faust.

Of course, the women of the North and the South who successfully guided themselves and their families through the war behaved in many different ways. Some women dedicated themselves to serving those in need, whereas others acted selfishly and paid little attention to the suffering that the war brought to others. But as Massey noted, most American women fell somewhere between these two extremes: "In varying degrees they possessed human frailties and virtues, and while willing to make sacrifices they found no reason for altering their usual way of life more than necessary. They saw no harm in participating in lively social functions or indulging an occasional selfish impulse, for as long as they contributed some of their time to charitable work why shouldn't they get some joy of out life?" Mary Chesnut, for example, was one of countless women who divided her time between volunteer service and social activities during the war years.

By the time the Civil War ended in 1865, it had forever changed the way that American women saw themselves. Many came away from the conflict with a greater sense of self-worth. In addition, the war made many women more likely to doubt the wisdom of their fathers and husbands, who had led the nation into a bloody conflict that ultimately cost more than six hundred thousand lives. But as Massey observed, the war's impact on individual women varied tremendously. "The Civil War was a mere episode in the lives of some women, a gay interlude [happy and exciting time] for a few, a profound experience for most, and a catastrophe for many," she wrote.

Subject matter of *Mary Chesnut's Civil War*

Mary Chesnut's Civil War spans the entire length of the American Civil War. The first diary entries are dated February 1861, when the first rumblings of war between North and South were being heard. The book then follows the progress of the war—and its impact on the author and the Southern society she loves so well—until the Confederacy finally goes down to defeat in 1865. Chesnut's diary concludes in July 1865, as she and her husband return to their South Carolina plantation and begin building new lives in the postwar South.

Mary Chesnut's Civil War

Edited by C. VANN WOODWARD

WINNER OF THE 1982 PULITZER PRIZE IN HISTORY

Cover of Mary Chesnut's Civil War. Painting of Mary Boykin Chesnut by Samuel Stillman Osgood. Reproduced by permission of Yale University Press.

The first diary entry in *Mary Chesnut's Civil War* is dated February 18, 1861. In these opening sentences, Chesnut sets the scene for readers by expressing her excitement and fear about the South's decision to leave the United States and form its own nation, called the Confederate States of America. "I do not allow myself vain regrets or sad foreboding [feeling of future disaster]," Chesnut writes. "This Southern Confederacy must be supported now by calm determination and cool brains. We have risked all, and we must play our best, for the stake is life or death."

As Chesnut continues her diary, she talks about the strong emotions that are felt all across the South as it prepares for war. "The war is making us all tenderly sentimental," she wrote on June 10, 1861. "No casualties yet, no real mourning, nobody hurt. So it is all parade, fife [a flute used in military songs], and fine feathers." But she admits that the excitement she feels is mingled with concern that the approaching war will bring great pain and sorrow, and she expresses surprise that more Southerners do not feel the same way. "There is no imagination here to forestall woe [delay grief], and only the excitement and wild awakening from everyday stagnant life are felt. That is, when one gets away from the two or three sensible men who are still left in the world."

The first battles of the Civil War erupt in the summer of 1861. Around this same period, Chesnut and her husband begin spending more of their time in the Confederate capital of Richmond, Virginia; a year later, they moved there. During this time, Chesnut's diary entries cover a great variety of subjects. For instance, she details her reasons for supporting secession, reacts to news of battles and political developments, and describes her volunteer work at army hospitals. She also bit-

terly condemns friends who do not do their part to support the Confederate army. "Shocked to hear that dear friends of mine refused to take work for the soldiers because their sempstresses [makers of clothing] had their winter clothes to make," she wrote on October 15, 1861. "I told them true patriotesses would be willing to wear the same clothes until our siege was raised [the war ends]. . . . They have seen no ragged, dirty, sick, and miserable soldiers lying in the hospital . . . but an awful lack of a proper change of clean clothes. They know nothing of the horrors of war. One has to see to believe. They take it easy and are not yet willing to make personal sacrifices. Time is coming when they will not be given a choice in the matter."

Chesnut also struggles with the issue of slavery in the pages of her diary. She admits that slavery is a "monstrous system," but repeatedly describes blacks in stereotypical terms. For example, she refers to black people as a lazy and simpleminded race that actually benefits from being cared for by their masters. "I say we are no better than our judges North—and *no worse*,"

The Confederate flag flies after the Confederacy captured Fort Sumter in South Carolina, marking the beginning of the American Civil War. Mary Chesnut started her Civil War diary shortly before this event took place. *Courtesy of the National Archives and Records Administration.*

Varina Davis, wife of Confederate president Jefferson Davis. Mary Chesnut and her husband were close friends with the couple. *Photograph by R. Wilhelm. Reproduced by permission of the Corbis Corporation.*

she declared on November 27, 1861. "We are human beings of the nineteenth century—and slavery has to go, of course. All that has been gained by it goes to the North and to negroes. The slave-owners, when they are good men and women, are the martyrs [victims]. And as far as I have seen, the people here are quite as good as anywhere else. I hate slavery. I even hate the harsh authority I see parents think it their duty to exercise *toward their children*."

But while Chesnut devotes considerable space to the Civil War, slavery, and Confederate politics, many of her diary entries from mid-1861 through 1863 concentrate on describing her daily interactions with the rich and influential people with whom she and her husband associated. In fact, Chesnut spent much of this period attending fancy dinner parties and other social events, where she dined and gossiped with many of the South's leading political figures. Over time, for instance, she became very close friends with Varina Davis (1826–1889), wife of Confederate president Jefferson Davis. She also emerged as an outspoken defender of President Davis, who was criticized for poor leadership by some Southerners.

But while Chesnut spends many pages describing the attitudes and activities of the Southern aristocracy, she always returns to the war. Chesnut's diary entries make it clear that she remains devoted to the Confederate cause. But as the war drags on, she expresses open doubt about the high price of forming a new nation. She claims that even if the Confederate army kills three Union soldiers for every Southern soldier killed, the death toll for the South will be too great. "Suppose we do all we hoped," she wrote on July 10, 1862. "Suppose we start up grand and free—a proud young republic. Think of all these young lives sacrificed! If three for one be killed, what comfort is that? What good will that do Mrs. Haynes or Mary DeSaussure? The best and the bravest of one generation swept away! Henry DeSaussure has left four sons to honor their father's memory and emulate [follow] his example. But those poor boys of between 18 and 20 years of age . . . they are washed away, literally, in a tide of blood. There is nothing to show they ever were on earth."

In May 1863, Union cavalry on a military mission rode within a few miles of Richmond. The news that the enemy had drawn so near to the Confederate capital alarmed many residents of the city, including Chesnut. In fact, she destroyed all her diary notes from August 1862 to May 1863 when she learned of their approach. In addition, she became so busy with hospital volunteer work and other activities during the summer of 1863 that she did not resume her diary until September 1863. At that time, she began writing down events from August 1862 to September 1863 from memory.

Some of these recollections were of enjoyable parties or witty conversations with friends, but others reflected the mounting death toll of the war. For example, at one point Chesnut recalls going to the funeral of Frank Hampton, a family friend who had been killed in the war: "How I wish I had not looked [into his coffin]!" she wrote. "I remember him so well in all the pride of his magnificent manhood. He died of a saber [sword] cut across his face and head and was utterly disfigured. Mrs. Singleton seemed convulsed with grief. In all my life I had never seen such bitter weeping. [Chesnut then recalls a pleasant week she spent with friends at the Hampton home before the war began]. . . . And now, it is only a few years, but nearly all that pleasant company are dead—and our world, the only world we cared for, literally kicked to pieces."

By 1864, Chesnut's diary entries reflect the increasingly desperate situation of the Confederacy. After more than three years of deadly warfare and sacrifice, Chesnut and other Southerners recognize that they are losing the war. This realization deeply saddens Chesnut, who had met many young Rebel soldiers at social events or in Confederate hospitals. "When I remember all the true-hearted, the lighthearted, the gay [happy] and gallant boys who have come laughing, singing, dancing in my way, in the three years past, I have looked into their brave young eyes and helped them as I could every way and then seen them no more forever," she wrote on July 26, 1864. "They lie stark and cold, dead upon the battlefield or moldering [decaying] away in hospitals or prisons—which is worse. I think, if I consider the long array of those bright youths and loyal men who have gone to their deaths almost before my very eyes, my heart might break, too. Is anything worth it? This fearful sacrifice—this awful penalty we pay for war?"

The last sections of *Mary Chesnut's Civil War* describe the final months of the conflict from the perspective of the South. Chesnut details the supply shortages that hit Richmond and other cities, draining the spirit of the residents. She also condemns Union general William T. Sherman (1820–1891) and his army, which tore a destructive path through the Confederacy's heartland during the war's final months. Finally, she expresses anger and sorrow when Northern forces overrun the South and claim victory in the spring of 1865. "They are everywhere, these Yankees—like red ants—like the locusts and frogs which were the plagues of Egypt," she declares. "A feeling of sadness hovers over me now, day and night, that no words of mine can express." Chesnut's diary then closes with two brief chapters that describe her return to the smoking ruins of her plantation home in South Carolina and her neighbors' efforts to resume their lives.

Style and themes in *Mary Chesnut's Civil War*

A wartime diary. Most of *Mary Chesnut's Civil War* is presented in a diary format. This day-by-day account of Chesnut's wartime feelings and experiences begins in February 1861, when the Confederacy was first being formed, and ends in the summer of 1865, with the Confederacy in ruins. But a major interruption in this diary format can be found from the summer of 1862 to the fall of 1863. During this time, the threat of Union invasion and Chesnut's busy schedule led her to temporarily abandon diary keeping. After the war, Chesnut filled in this fifteen-month gap by writing down her memories of that period. This section of the book more closely resembles a memoir than a diary, but it has the same tone as the rest of the work.

Chesnut's book is filled with commentary on many different issues and events of the Civil War era. But there are several subjects that she returns to time and time again. These subjects—slavery, relationships between men and women, and the war against the North—are the primary themes of *Mary Chesnut's Civil War.*

Chesnut's conflicted feelings about slavery. Chesnut repeatedly criticizes the practice of slavery in the pages of her diary. She refers to slavery as a "monstrous system" and expresses amazement that some foolish Southerners "still believe negroes to be property." She even admits at one point that if her worst fears come true and the South is defeated in the Civil War, at least she will be able to take comfort in the knowledge that slavery has been abolished.

But even though Chesnut declares her hatred for slavery on numerous occasions, she continued to benefit from slave labor throughout the war. As historian C. Vann Woodward noted in the introduction to *Mary Chesnut's Civil War,* "She was the wife of the heir to one of the great slave estates of her time, a product and an elite member of a slave society, an intimate [close friend] of its chief defenders and champions, and a close friend of President and Mrs. Jefferson Davis." In fact, Chesnut freely admitted that she enjoyed all the personal attention she received from her slaves. In addition, she often described individual master-slave relationships in positive terms. For example, she related many stories of slaves who were loyal to their masters and happy with their enslavement. She recognized that some slavemasters were cruel to their slaves. But she also insisted that most Southern slaveowners treated their slaves with kindness and actually made sacrifices on their behalf.

Chesnut's diary also reflects the common belief—seen in both Southern and Northern communities of the Civil War era—that blacks were inferior to whites. She often describes slaves she personally knows in positive terms, but she uses racist language when referring to black people in general. For example, she describes the black race as lazy, dirty, and "ill smelling by nature" and states that they lack the intelligence and the morals of white people. She also criticizes the physical appearance of blacks and mulattoes—people of mixed white and black heritage. For example, in a November 25, 1861, diary entry, Chesnut describes a woman named Martha Adamson as "a beautiful mulatress" (a woman with one white parent and one black parent). But the author then adds that black and mulatto people cannot compare with whites in the area of

Chesnut's Words Used in Famous Documentary

In 1990, the Public Broadcasting System (PBS) broadcast *The Civil War,* a nine-part documentary on the conflict that raged across America from 1861 to 1865. This thirteen-hour mini-series, which was produced by filmmaker Ken Burns (1953–), was a critical and popular success. Burns retold the story of the war through the use of historical photographs, Civil War–era music, and contemporary film footage of Civil War battlefields. He also enlisted well-known actors like Sam Waterston (1940–), Jason Robards (1922–2000), and Morgan Freeman (1937–) to read excerpts from diaries, letters, and speeches written by soldiers, generals, politicians, and civilians during the years of bloody conflict. One of the most frequently quoted Civil War figures in Burns's documentary was Mary Chesnut. Burns repeatedly used excerpts from her diary because he felt that she was a bright and observant woman whose comments reflected both the hopes and fears of the South during the war years.

*The Civil War'*s nine episodes—"The Cause," "A Very Bloody Affair," "Forever Free," "Simply Murder," "The Universe of Battle," "Valley of the Shadow of Death," "Most Hallowed Ground," "War Is All Hell," and "The Better Angels of Our Nature"— provide a chronological account of the war. The series begins by explaining the issues that led to Southern secession, then recounts the four long years of bloody struggle that battered the nation. It con-

Filmmaker Ken Burns. *Photograph by Lee Marriner. Reproduced by permission of AP/Wide World Photos.*

cludes by detailing the war's last days and describing the postwar lives of Americans whose lives were forever changed by the conflict, from generals and statesmen to ordinary soldiers.

Burns believes that the tremendous popularity of his documentary series can be traced to the lasting impact of the war on American society. "I think we continually need to understand how important an event the war was—how defining, how central to who we are," Burns has stated. "Everything that came before it led up to it, and everything of importance to this country—at least up to 1940—was a consequence of it. Even now there's an echo of the war, however faint, in almost everyone's life."

physical beauty. She states that even Adamson is only "as good-looking as they [blacks and mulattoes] ever are to me. I have never seen a mule as handsome as a horse—and I know I never will—no matter how I lament and sympathize with its undeserved mule condition."

Chesnut criticizes society's treatment of women. Another theme that pops up regularly in Mary Chesnut's book is her frustration with the powerlessness of women in American society. She expresses particularly strong anger toward Southern traditions and laws, which place nearly all authority in the hands of men and grant women few freedoms. "South Carolina as a rule does not think it necessary for women to have any existence out of their pantries or nurseries," Chesnut writes in a February 16, 1864, diary entry. "If they have none [no children], let them nurse the bare walls. But for men! The pleasures of all the world are reserved!"

As Chesnut's diary continues, the author even compares the circumstances in which she and other white women live to that of slavery. "In a dozen ways she equated the plight of women with that of slaves," wrote Woodward. "They were bought and sold, deprived of their liberty, their property, their civil rights, and the equal protection of the law, humiliated and reduced to abject [miserable] dependency" on men. This unequal status is particularly bothersome to Chesnut because she believes that many men are foolish, arrogant, and ignorant. For example, in a December 8, 1861, passage, she expresses amazement at "how men can go blustering around—making everybody uncomfortable simply to show that they are masters—and we only women and children at their mercy."

But Chesnut saved her harshest criticism for white Southern men who acted as if they were virtuous and moral people, instructing their wives and daughters on proper behavior, only to sneak off at night and force their women slaves to have sex with them. In an August 26, 1861, entry, for example, Chesnut ridicules the slaveholder who keeps such slaves "under the same roof" as "his lovely white wife and his beautiful and accomplished daughters": "He holds his head as high and poses as the model of all human virtues to these poor women whom God and the laws have given him. From the height of his awful majesty he scolds and thunders at them, as if he never did wrong in his life."

War of Rebellion. In *Mary Chesnut's Civil War,* the author refers again and again to events on distant Civil War battlefields. As she follows the progress of the war—rejoicing in Confederate victories and expressing sorrow over Confederate defeats—her journal shows how the entire South felt as the war unfolded. Her diary thus reflects the strong emotions that coursed through the South during the conflict, which Southerners called the "War of Rebellion." In fact, many of Chesnut's words reflect the bitterness that the South felt toward the North before, during, and after the war. Like many Southerners, Chesnut believed that Northerners adopted a superior moral tone on the issue of slavery. She also shared the widespread Southern feeling that Northerners did not really understand how slavery was practiced in their communities. She and other people of the South also resented the North's "interference" with their way of life. As a result, Chesnut peppered her diary with remarks that showed her intense dislike for the "Yankees" of the North.

Research and Activity Ideas

1) Mary Chesnut was a smart and educated woman, yet she held many views that are now widely seen as ignorant. Name a few of the mistaken beliefs that she held about the world around her. Why do you think she felt the way she did? How have American beliefs about those issues changed over the years?

2) Mary Chesnut and other Southern women of the pre–Civil War era led pampered lives in some ways. But in other respects, they had very little control over their lives. In what ways were their lives easy? In what ways were they difficult? Do you think that Chesnut's comparison of womanhood to slavery was accurate?

3) At the end of the war, the Chesnuts' home and most of their belongings were destroyed by the Union army. Do you feel sorry for Mary Chesnut and other Southerners who lost homes and property during the war? Or do you think that they deserved to suffer these losses?

Related Titles

Burns, Ken, director. *The Civil War.* Walpole, NH: Florentine Films/PBS, 1990. *This nine-part documentary film series tells the story of the Civil War through letters, photographs, and newspaper articles.*

Chang, Ina. *A Separate Battle: Women in the Civil War.* New York: Lodestar Books, 1991. Reprint, New York: Puffin Books, 1996. *A nonfiction book about the hardships of the home front and the contributions of women on both sides of the Civil War.*

Meltzer, Milton. *Voices from the Civil War.* New York: Crowell, 1989. *A collection of diaries, letters, speeches, and articles that tell the story of the Civil War from many different perspectives.*

Where to Learn More About . . .

Mary Boykin Chesnut

DeCredico, Mary A. *Mary Boykin Chesnut: A Confederate Woman's Life.* Madison, WI: Madison House, 1996.

Muhlenfeld, Elisabeth. *Mary Boykin Chesnut: A Biography.* Baton Rouge: Louisiana State University Press, 1981.

University of North Carolina at Chapel Hill Libraries. "Mary Boykin Miller Chesnut, 1823–1886." *Documenting the American South.* [Online] http://docsouth.unc.edu/chesnut/menu.html (accessed on August 23, 2001).

Woodward, C. Vann. Introduction to *Mary Chesnut's Civil War.* New Haven, CT: Yale University Press, 1981.

Women during the Civil War Era

Faust, Drew Gilpin. *Mothers of Invention: Women of the Slaveholding South in the American Civil War.* Chapel Hill: University of North Carolina Press, 1996.

Fox-Genovese, Elizabeth. *Within the Plantation Household: Black and White Women of the Old South.* Chapel Hill: University of North Carolina Press, 1988.

Massey, Mary Elizabeth. *Women in the Civil War.* Lincoln: University of Nebraska Press, 1994.

North Star to Freedom

By Gena K. Gorrell

North Star to Freedom: The Story of the Underground Railroad is a nonfiction book that presents the history of slavery in North America as well as the efforts of brave people to end it. The main focus of the book is the Underground Railroad. The Underground Railroad was not actually a railroad. It was a secret network of homes and barns scattered across the American South. Through this network, it is estimated that tens of thousands of escaped slaves received help on their dangerous journey to freedom in the northern United States and Canada.

The author of *North Star to Freedom,* Canadian author Gena K. Gorrell (1946–), was raised as a Quaker. Members of the Society of Friends religious group—also known as the Quakers—were some of the first people in North America to speak out against slavery. Quakers strongly believed in the equality of all people, no matter what their race or background. Therefore, they viewed slavery as immoral. Gorrell's native Canada outlawed slavery before the United States and became an important destination for runaway slaves. Gorrell's background as a Quaker and a Canadian led to her interest in writing about the Underground Railroad.

Biography of author Gena K. Gorrell

Gena Kinton Gorrell was born in 1946. She was raised as a Quaker in Toronto, Ontario, Canada. Gorrell worked as a computer programmer for several years and then became an editor at a Canadian publishing house. In the 1990s, she quit her job and began working as a freelance editor in order to spend more time writing. Gorrell published her first book, *North Star to Freedom,* in 1996. She is also the author of two other nonfiction books for young adults: *Catching Fire: The Story of Firefighting* (1999) and *Heart and Soul: The Story of Florence Nightingale* (2000).

Historical background of *North Star to Freedom*

The Underground Railroad operated in some form for about fifty years, from the early 1800s until the start of the American Civil War (1861–65) in 1861. Since its activities took place in secret, the total number of "passengers" transported on the Underground Railroad is not known. But historians estimate that approximately fifty thousand slaves may have reached freedom in the northern United States or Canada using this method.

The Underground Railroad mostly operated in the slave states that bordered the free states of the North. It did not have a very strong presence in the Deep South, because slaves who escaped from plantations there would have had to travel too far to reach the northern United States or Canada. Instead, these runaways usually tried to blend in with the free black populations in large Southern cities. Some fugitive slaves in the Deep South hid in remote regions like the Florida Everglades or went to Mexico, where slavery was not allowed.

Blacks living in the North—including both free blacks and former slaves—played an important role in operating the Underground Railroad. Many blacks who had used the secret network to escape later became "conductors"—people who guided other slaves to freedom. One of the most famous conductors was Harriet Tubman (1820–1913), who escaped from slavery in 1849 and helped more than three hundred fellow slaves reach freedom over the next decade (see box). White abolitionists (people who fought to end slavery) took part in the Underground Railroad as well. All the people who aided

slaves on their journey to freedom risked harsh punishment if their activities were discovered.

The slaves who traveled on the Underground Railroad showed great courage as well. Before they decided to escape, most fugitive slaves had never been more than a few miles away from the plantations where they lived. Many did not know how to read or follow a map. Some only knew that they needed to head in the general direction of the North Star. As the Underground Railroad became more successful in helping slaves to escape, slave owners organized patrols to capture runaways and frighten other slaves who might be thinking about leaving. Some owners offered large rewards for the return of their property. Slaves who dared to risk escape knew that they could be severely beaten or even killed if they were captured.

Even slaves who reached the North were not entirely safe. They could always be captured by a slave catcher—a person hired to find fugitive slaves and return them to their masters. In 1842,

Harriet Tubman (far left) stands with six slaves she guided to freedom along the Underground Railroad. *Courtesy of the Library of Congress.*

Harriet Tubman

Harriet Tubman was one of the most famous conductors on the Underground Railroad. After escaping from slavery herself, she made nineteen dangerous trips into slave territory and helped more than three hundred slaves gain their freedom.

Tubman was born on a plantation in Maryland around 1820. When she was seven years old, her master hired her out to a cruel woman named Miss Susan. Tubman took care of Miss Susan's baby and did household chores. Miss Susan beat her whenever the baby cried or the house was not clean enough. These beatings left scars that would remain visible for the rest of Tubman's life.

After returning to her master's plantation, Tubman went to work in the cotton fields. She dreamed about running away, but she did not know where to go and could not read a map. When Tubman's master died in 1849, she learned that she and the other slaves would be sold to pay the plantation's debts. Since there was little market for slaves in Maryland, they would likely be taken to the Deep South to pick cotton. Tubman decided that the time had come for her to run away.

Tubman left the plantation late one night and went to a house that she had heard was part of the Underground Railroad. She received directions to the next station. She traveled secretly for the next several nights with the help of people who opposed slavery. She paid careful attention to her route so that she could eventually return and rescue her family. Finally, after a journey of one hundred miles, Tubman crossed the border into Pennsylvania, where slavery was not allowed. "There was such a glory over everything," she recalled. "I felt like I was in heaven."

Tubman settled in Philadelphia and took a job washing dishes in a hotel. She saved her money in hopes of returning to Maryland and bringing her family to free-

a U.S. Supreme Court ruling made the job of capturing runaway slaves in the North more difficult. In the case of *Prigg v. Pennsylvania,* the court said that slave owners could recapture their slaves in free states but that they could not break the law or use illegal violence to do it. The ruling also said that people in the Northern states did not have to help slave owners retrieve their property.

Southerners were very angry about the Supreme Court's decision. They felt that the ruling violated their property rights. They immediately began trying to pass a tough new fugitive

Harriet Tubman. *Reproduced by permission of the Granger Collection Ltd.*

dom. Tubman made her first trip to the South in 1850 and helped her brothers and her elderly parents escape from slavery. She made a total of nineteen trips into slave territory over the next ten years. Each time she made the dangerous journey, she risked being captured and returned to her owner's estate. At one point, there was a huge reward of $12,000 offered for her capture.

When the Civil War began in 1861, Tubman looked for ways to help the Union cause. She served Union troops as a cook, a nurse, a laundress, and a spy during the war. In July 1863, she led a group of boats containing black soldiers on a raid up a South Carolina river. They ended up capturing Confederate supplies and freeing 750 slaves, many of whom later joined the Union army.

After the war ended in 1865, Tubman moved to Auburn, New York. Two years later, a friend of hers named Sarah Bradford published a book called *Scenes in the Life of Harriet Tubman*. Tubman used the money from sales of the book to build schools to educate freed slaves and hospitals to treat sick and elderly blacks. Harriet Tubman died on March 10, 1913, at the age of ninety-three.

slave law that would help them catch and reclaim runaway slaves. The eventual result of their efforts was the Fugitive Slave Act of 1850. This law gave slave owners sweeping new powers to capture escaped slaves who had reached free territory. It also required Northerners to help them catch runaway slaves and established severe penalties for anyone who provided the slaves with food, shelter, or any other kind of assistance.

Slave owners were pleased with the new Fugitive Slave Act. But people in the North resented it. Before long, slave catch-

Illustration depicts fugitive slaves fleeing on the Underground Railroad.
Reproduced by permission of Archive Photos.

ers began taking advantage of the law to capture free blacks in the North and force them into slavery. Such abuses of the law ended up increasing Northern opposition to slavery. "The pitiful spectacle of helpless blacks being seized in the streets and dragged off to slavery could unsettle the most prejudiced northern white," Jeffrey Rogers Hummel wrote in *Emancipating Slaves, Enslaving Free Men.* "Northern mobs, which once had directed their fury at abolitionists, now attacked slave catchers, broke into jails, and rescued fugitive slaves. . . . The national government tried vigorously to prosecute the lawbreakers responsible for such defiance, but northern juries refused to convict."

The success of the Underground Railroad made slave owners desperate to capture runaway slaves. But the law that was intended to help them only ended up making matters worse. The Fugitive Slave Act made it impossible for people who supported slavery and people who opposed slavery to reach a compromise. It increased the tension between North and South that led to the Civil War.

Subject matter of *North Star to Freedom*

North Star to Freedom provides readers with an overview of slavery and the struggle against it. The main focus of the book is the Underground Railroad. This secret network of abolitionists helped slaves escape from their masters and settle in the northern United States and Canada, where slavery was not allowed. "Some slaves made the dangerous trip [to freedom in the North] with no assistance except an occasional scrap of food or word of advice from someone they happened to meet along the way," Gorrell writes in her introduction to *North Star to Freedom.* "But others were helped by a secret network of people, both black and white, who together helped runaways find their way to freedom. The secret network was known as the Underground Railroad. This is the story of how it worked and of some of the people who took part in it."

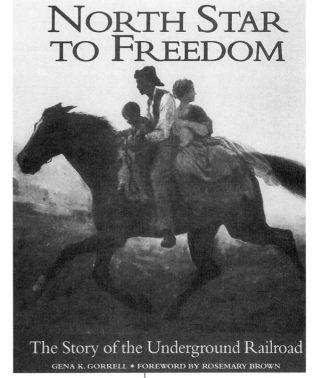

The Story of the Underground Railroad

GENA K. GORRELL * FOREWORD BY ROSEMARY BROWN

Cover of *North Star to Freedom.* "A Ride for Liberty— The Fugitive Slaves." Painting by Eastman Johnson, from the Brooklyn Museum. Reproduced by permission of Dell Publishing Co.

In the first chapter, Gorrell discusses the history of slavery and how it spread to North America in the 1600s. The second chapter tells how black people were captured in African villages and taken to other parts of the world to become slaves. In some cases, people were captured and sold into slavery by fellow Africans from rival tribes. Once they collected enough black people, slave traders packed them into the cargo holds of ships and sailed across the oceans for several weeks. Many Africans died of disease, starvation, or fear during this time. Others committed suicide rather than become slaves. Once they arrived at their destination, they were sold at auctions like furniture or other possessions.

The third chapter of *North Star to Freedom* talks about slavery during America's colonial period in the 1700s. During this time, an entire society was built upon the practice of slavery, particularly in the southern colonies. Slaves provided a cheap source of labor for large farms that grew cotton and tobacco. By using slaves, white property owners could farm large areas of land at very little cost. As a result, they became very wealthy and enjoyed an elegant lifestyle. Over time, slavery became very important to the South's economy and way of life.

But the plantation system in the South was based on the idea that blacks were not people. According to Gorrell, white landowners were able to look at blacks and say, "They're not like us. They don't look like us or act like us. They don't seem to think the way we think, so they obviously don't feel the way we feel. *Their race must not be as good as ours.*" Whites used the idea that blacks were inferior as an excuse for slavery. But even though most slave owners thought they were superior to their slaves, they spent a great deal of time and effort trying to keep blacks in slavery. For example, they tried to prevent slaves from learning to read and write. "After all, people who read books and newspapers might come across all sorts of dangerous ideas—ideas about freedom and equality," Gorrell notes.

The fourth chapter covers early efforts to abolish (put an end to) slavery. As early as 1688, Gorrell explains, white people who belonged to the Quaker religious group began speaking out against the practice. By the 1700s, slavery started disappearing in America's northern colonies. One reason was that the climate in the North was not as good for farming as in the South. The North's economy was based on manufacturing, so people did not have a strong need for slaves. In addition, many free black people lived and worked in northern cities. The contributions of these people made it difficult for whites to consider them inferior. But slavery continued to exist in the South, where it was important to the region's economy and way of life.

In the fifth chapter, Gorrell talks about the difficult journey escaped slaves made to freedom. As valuable property, slaves were watched very closely. In order to prevent escapes, black people in the South were not allowed to ride trains, cross bridges, or travel anywhere without a pass signed by their masters. Those who were caught trying to escape were punished severely. Despite the danger, however, many slaves attempted to escape, and some reached safety in the northern United States or Canada. Gorrell includes several true stories about slaves who took the risk to find freedom.

Scene depicting African Americans escaping from slavery. *"A Bold Stroke for Freedom." Engraving from the book* The Underground Railroad, *by William Still. Reproduced by permission of the Corbis Corporation.*

Gorrell also introduces the people who helped fugitive slaves on their difficult journey. She talks about how these people gradually became bolder and more organized in their work until they had formed the Underground Railroad. "As the people helping the runaways got to know who was sympathetic and who wasn't, who could be trusted and who couldn't, they became more confident," Gorrell states. "They started planning ahead, planning together, looking for safer ways to guide more runaways northward. Slowly a network of rescue was growing—a secret network of people who dared to put themselves at risk for what they knew was right. It had no single leader, no official existence, no formal organization. But it would become a legend."

Chapter six provides readers with information about the Underground Railroad. It first began forming in the early 1800s in the slave states that bordered the North, such as Missouri, Kentucky, and Maryland. Gorrell defines several terms associated with the railroad. "The *conductors* were people who

THE ROUTES OF THE UNDERGROUND RAILROAD

Maine

Minnesota

Vermont

New Hampshire

Wisconsin

Massachusetts

Michigan

New York

Connecticut

Rhode Island

Unorganized Territory

Iowa

Pennsylvania

New Jersey

Illinois

Ohio

Delaware

Indiana

Maryland

Missouri

Kentucky

Virginia

Tennessee

North Carolina

Arkansas

South Carolina

Alabama

Georgia

Texas

Mississippi

Florida

Louisiana

Free state

Slave state

A map of the eastern U.S. shows the routes of the Underground Railroad. Areas shaded light grey represent free states and dark grey represent slave states. Heavy black arrows indicate railroad routes. *The Gale Group.*

met fugitive slaves—*passengers*—and guided them along their way, giving them directions, leading them on foot or by horse, or smuggling them in carts and carriages. The *stations* were places where runaways could stop and rest, getting a meal and a night's sleep, and perhaps fresh clothing or other help. A station might be a barn or a church, a lonely farmhouse, or a secret room in a fashionable town home. Stations were run by *stationmasters*. Conductors and stationmasters were often free blacks or poor farmers, but they could also be wealthy, well-known citizens." Gorrell also talks about how the railroad managed to remain hidden. She describes some of the ways conductors tricked slave owners who came looking for their property.

In chapter seven, Gorrell relates the stories of more runaway slaves. Some of these brave people later spoke and wrote about their lives in order to help others understand the evil of slavery. The next chapter deals with the abolitionist movement in the North. Gorrell discusses how the movement started and how it grew. One of the most important factors in increasing antislavery feelings in the North was the Fugitive Slave Act of 1850. This law said that blacks in the North could be captured and returned to slavery in the South. In addition, it required people in the North to help slave owners retrieve their slaves.

The Fugitive Slave Act made slavery seem more real to many Northerners. They could ignore slavery when it was practiced hundreds of miles away, but not when they saw black people being captured and dragged away in their cities and towns. "Now respected black citizens—craftsmen, publishers, business owners—could be seized from their homes and sent in chains back to the cotton fields, and their friends and neighbors could do nothing to help them," Gorrell explains. "Furthermore, the law said that captured blacks had no right to appeal the capture. Their supposed owners simply had to declare that the captured blacks were escaped slaves. Even if the declaration was untrue—even if the blacks had bought their freedom, even if they were free-born blacks who were being mistaken for someone else—they had no chance to prove their case. This was an intolerable injustice, and it drew even more northerners to the abolitionist cause."

In chapter nine of *North Star to Freedom*, Gorrell tells about other events that increased the bitter divisions between the North and the South over slavery. One of these events was the 1852 publication of *Uncle Tom's Cabin,* a novel by abolitionist Harriet Beecher Stowe (1811–1896). This book was one of the first to present black characters as real people with the same hopes and dreams as whites. It brought the horrors of slavery to life and inspired thousands of people to join the abolitionist movement (see box).

Uncle Tom's Cabin

The 1852 novel *Uncle Tom's Cabin,* by abolitionist writer Harriet Beecher Stowe, is the most important antislavery book in American history. Stowe was inspired to write the novel by her anger over the Fugitive Slave Act of 1850. This law gave slave owners sweeping new powers to capture and reclaim escaped slaves. It also required people in the North to assist the slave owners in retrieving their property. The Fugitive Slave Act increased antislavery feelings across the North and encouraged thousands of people to join the abolitionist movement.

Stowe's novel follows the lives of several slaves who work for a cruel man named Simon Legree in the South. Through the experiences of these slaves, the author creates a powerful image of the evils of slavery. In order to add realistic details to the story, Stowe read several books on slavery, including *American Slavery as It Is* by Theodore Dwight Weld (1803–1895). She also exchanged letters with former slave and abolitionist Frederick Douglass (1817–1895).

Uncle Tom's Cabin was one of the first books to present black characters as human beings with the same strengths and weaknesses as other people. It raised readers' awareness of the terrible conditions in which most slaves lived, and it increased people's

Advertisement for the book *Uncle Tom's Cabin.* *Public domain.*

sympathy and understanding toward them. In this way, it helped convince countless Northerners that slavery was wrong.

Uncle Tom's Cabin sold more than two million copies in the ten years following its publication, making it the best-selling book ever up to that time. Some historians claim that, by making people in the North less willing to compromise on the issue of slavery, the book helped cause the Civil War. In fact, President Abraham Lincoln once called Stowe "the little lady who wrote the book that made this big war."

Gorrell also discusses the formation of the Republican political party in 1854. The Republican Party opposed slavery and was determined to prevent it from spreading beyond the

Southern states where it was already allowed. In 1860, the Republicans chose Abraham Lincoln (1809–1865) as their candidate for president of the United States. A relatively unknown lawyer from Illinois, Lincoln strongly opposed slavery. But he favored eliminating the practice gradually rather than outlawing it immediately. Still, the Southern states worried that a president who opposed slavery could not represent their interests. When Lincoln won the election, several Southern states seceded (withdrew) from the Union and formed their own country that allowed slavery, the Confederate States of America, also called the Confederacy.

In chapter ten of her book, Gorrell talks about the rights that were granted to black people in Canada. America's northern neighbor began phasing out slavery in the late 1700s. In 1793, officials in the part of Canada that eventually became the province of Ontario passed a law saying that any slaves who entered their territory would be set free automatically. Beginning in 1826, the Canadian government formally refused to return any fugitive slaves to the United States. Although black settlers in Canada still encountered prejudice, they were granted equal rights under the law. For this reason, Canada was the preferred destination for many American slaves traveling on the Underground Railroad.

Chapter eleven of *North Star to Freedom* covers the American Civil War and its effect on slavery. In 1862, President Lincoln issued the Emancipation Proclamation. This document declared that slaves held in the Confederate states would become free on the first day of 1863. Of course, since the Confederate states considered themselves a separate country, they claimed that Lincoln had no right to make rules for them and refused to honor the proclamation. It was only in 1865, when the North finally won the Civil War, that slaves in the South were freed. Then slavery was outlawed across America through an amendment to the U.S. Constitution.

Gorrell concludes her book by talking about the problems that continue to face African Americans in North America today. "Blacks would suffer many years of mean and unfair treatment, and sometimes violence, as they worked to overcome the long-lasting effects of slavery. Today, in the United States and Canada, problems and prejudices still remain," she explains. "But while the story of slavery is an ugly one, it is finally a story of justice overcoming injustice. It's a story of wrongs being made right—not easily, not quickly, but through the determination of men and women, black and white."

Style and themes in *North Star to Freedom*

North Star to Freedom is arranged chronologically. It begins with the origins of slavery, charts the growth of opposition to the practice, traces the history of the Underground Railroad, and ends with the abolition of slavery in the United States during the Civil War. The book contains numerous photographs, paintings, and historical posters that give readers visual images of the issues it covers. Gorrell also includes many personal stories about slaves and the people who helped free them.

Each chapter in *North Star to Freedom* begins with a brief description of a situation that might have happened to a slave. These descriptions help readers imagine themselves in the position of a slave and understand the issues that are covered in the chapter. For example, the situation described in the introduction to the book concerns a child who is awakened in the middle of the night by his mother. It soon becomes clear that the child is a slave and that his mother has decided to try to escape. The child has been sleeping in a rickety shed with other slaves. He is confused about what is happening as his mother tells him to be quiet and follow her. His mother finally tells him that they are running away to find freedom in Canada. She is not sure how to get there, but she plans to follow the North Star. As they begin their long journey toward freedom, she tells him: "Beginning tonight—beginning the minute we walked out of that shed back there—we're free. And we're not ever going to be slaves again."

Although *North Star to Freedom* includes many details about the terrible practice of slavery, the main message of the book is a positive one. Gorrell emphasizes the courage of the slaves who attempted to escape and of the people who helped them reach freedom. She argues that the fight to end slavery showed the basic strength and determination of the people involved in it. She presents the Underground Railroad as an example of the power of ordinary people to correct the problems in their society and make the world a better place.

Research and Activity Ideas

1) Create a map of some of the most commonly used routes on the Underground Railroad. Are there any stations near where you live? Pick three states that allowed slavery. Measure the distance from a central point in each state to the nearest spot where escaped slaves could reach freedom.

2) What gave some slaves the courage to attempt to escape on the Underground Railroad? What gave the conductors the courage to help the slaves reach freedom? Choose moments from the book in which each group shows courage.

3) Imagine that you are a small farmer who lives along an Underground Railroad route. Will you help escaped slaves who pass by? List the positive and negative things about becoming involved in the Underground Railroad. Research the Fugitive Slave Act of 1850 and the punishments it established for people who helped escaped slaves. How does this affect your decision?

4) The leaders of the abolitionist movement and the people involved in the Underground Railroad inspired many others to speak out against racial injustice a century later. Research the life of a prominent member of the American civil rights movement, such as Rosa Parks (1913–), Martin Luther King Jr.(1929–1968), Medgar Evers (1925–1963), or Malcolm X (1925–1965). Write a brief biography emphasizing that person's contributions in the fight to gain equal rights for African Americans.

Related Titles

Ayres, Katherine. *North by Night: A Story of the Underground Railroad.* New York: Delacorte Press, 1998. *A collection of diaries and letters describe the efforts of a sixteen-year-old Ohio girl to help slaves on the Underground Railroad.*

Collier, James Lincoln, and Christopher Collier. *Jump Ship to Freedom.* New York: Delacorte Press, 1981. *A young boy steals documentation from a captain to ensure freedom from slavery for himself and his mother, but the angry captain forces the boy onto a ship headed to the West Indies, which means certain slavery.*

Levine, Ellen. *Freedom's Children: Young Civil Rights Activists Tell Their Own Stories.* New York: Putnam, 2000. *A collection of thirty oral histories from the 1950s and 1960s that show African Americans' continuing struggle for equal rights.*

McKissack, Patricia C. *A Picture of Freedom: The Diary of Clotee, a Slave Girl, Belmont Plantation.* New York: Scholastic, 1997. *A story told from the perspective of an African American girl who must decide whether to escape to freedom or remain a slave and become a conductor on the Underground Railroad.*

Paulsen, Gary. *Nightjohn.* New York: Delacorte Press, 1993. *A novel about a former slave who gives up his freedom to return to the South and teach other slaves to read and write.*

Thomas, Velma M. *Lest We Forget: The Passage from Africa to Slavery and Emancipation.* New York: Crown Trade Paperbacks, 1997. *Tells the story of slavery in the United States in words and historical photographs.*

Turner, Glennette Tilley. *Running for Our Lives.* New York: Holiday House, 1994. *The story of a black family's dangerous journey to freedom in Canada on the Underground Railroad.*

Where to Learn More About . . .

The Underground Railroad

Blockson, Charles L. *The Underground Railroad.* New York: Prentice Hall, 1987.

Burns, Bree. *Harriet Tubman and the Fight against Slavery.* New York: Chelsea Juniors, 1992.

Haskins, Jim. *Get on Board: The Story of the Underground Railroad.* New York: Scholastic, 1993.

Hummel, Jeffrey Rogers. *Emancipating Slaves, Enslaving Free Men.* Chicago: Open Court Publishing, 1996.

McMullen, Kate. *The Story of Harriet Tubman: Conductor of the Underground Railroad.* New York: Dell, 1991. Reprint, Milwaukee: Gareth Stevens, 1997.

Menare Foundation's North Star Website. [Online] http://www.ugrr.org (accessed on August 30, 2001).

National Geographic Online. *The Underground Railroad.* [Online] http://www.nationalgeographic.com/features/99/railroad (accessed on August 30, 2001).

National Park Service. *Aboard the Underground Railroad: A National Register Travel Itinerary.* [Online] http://www.cr.nps.gov/nr/travel/underground/ugrrhome.htm (accessed on August 30, 2001).

The Underground Railroad Site. [Online] http://education.ucdavis.edu/NEW/STC/lesson/socstud/railroad/contents.htm (accessed on August 30, 2001).

Till Victory Is Won

Written by Zak Mettger

Z ak Mettger's nonfiction book *Till Victory Is Won: Black Soldiers in the Civil War* provides a detailed account of the struggle that black Americans waged to gain a place in the Union army. It also shows what black soldiers experienced—both on and off the battlefield—over the course of the American Civil War (1861–65). Finally, the book explains how the bravery of black Union troops helped put all black Americans on the path to freedom.

Biography of author Zak Mettger

Zak Mettger was born on July 11, 1950, in Washington, D.C. She was the oldest of two daughters born to Philip Mettger, an administrator, and Ursula Mettger, a secretary. Philip Mettger was a founder of the Governmental Affairs Institute, a Washington-based organization that arranged for government officials from around the world to visit the United States to learn about democracy.

Mettger grew up in Somerset, Maryland, a small town near Washington, D.C. She attended Western Junior High

Zak Mettger, author of *Till Victory Is Won*. *Reproduced by permission of Zak Mettger.*

School and Bethesda–Chevy Chase High School, from which she graduated in 1968. She then enrolled in Earlham College, a small liberal arts college in Richmond, Indiana. "Like so many other kids of my generation, I wound up dropping out of school partway through my junior year," recalled Mettger in correspondence with *Experiencing the American Civil War*. "I'd like to say I spent the next year discovering myself and my calling, but no such luck; mostly, I floundered." Eventually, however, she returned to college. She enrolled in California State College at Sonoma, where she graduated with a bachelor's degree in 1974.

Mettger continued her education at the University of Maryland, earning a master's degree in social work in 1980. During this period, she also began working as a writer. "I became a writer mostly by accident," she said in an interview for *Experiencing the American Civil War*. "I discovered during a graduate school practicum [teaching program] at a battered women's shelter that I preferred writing newsletters, educational materials, and fundraising proposals to the counseling and other forms of traditional social work I was supposedly training for." By the early 1980s, Mettger was writing reports, newsletters, brochures, magazine articles, and other materials for several nonprofit organizations.

Mettger established herself as an author in 1994, when she published two books targeted at young adult audiences. These two books covered different aspects of America's Civil War era. Her book *Till Victory Is Won: Black Soldiers in the Civil War* provided readers with information on the struggles and triumphs of black Union troops during the conflict. It proved very popular with young adult audiences and received the Carter G. Woodson Book Award from the National Council for Social Studies. Mettger's other 1994 book, *Reconstruction: America After the Civil War,* explained events that took place in the American South from 1865 to 1877. During this period, known as Reconstruction, America's Southern states and citizens began rebuilding their economy and way of life under the supervision of the national government.

Mettger recalls her work on the two Civil War works as a tiring but rewarding experience. "I spent months in the Library of Congress and other research institutions and lots of time on the phone, tracking down obscure primary source material [journals, letters, and articles written by people of the Civil War era] and period photographs," she said. "Then I tackled the job of condensing thousands of pages of materials into a one-hundred-page narrative that was both historically accurate and compelling enough to engage ten- to fourteen-year-olds. The eighteen months it took me to complete these two book projects—I was also working full time—were the most exhausting and exhilarating of my professional life. I had never felt so intellectually engaged. I was pleased and proud when the books came out in 1994 to favorable reviews, both from professional sources and a number of young friends. Even more exciting, I knew I had found work that joined my desire to write and my need for intellectual challenge with my desire to contribute to society, in this case by illuminating [clarifying] history, politics, and social issues . . . for children through the lives of ordinary people."

After completing *Till Victory Is Won* and *Reconstruction*, Mettger joined with author Elias Vlanton (1951–) to write a book called *Who Killed George Polk?* The book, published in 1996, examines the mysterious circumstances behind the death of George Polk (1913–1948), a famous newspaper reporter of the 1940s. Mettger then agreed to serve as coeditor of a series of books to be published by the New Press. The series, called the *Justice Talking* series, will debate controversial issues in modern American society, such as school vouchers and Internet censorship. In addition, Mettger continues to write materials for nonprofit organizations that are working to solve social problems in America.

Historical background of *Till Victory Is Won*

During the first century of the United States' existence, America's Northern and Southern regions became entangled in a bitter disagreement over the issue of slavery. The nation's Northern states thought it was an immoral practice, and they passed firm laws against slaveholding. But the agriculture-based economy of the South was heavily dependent on the physical labor of slaves, and many Southerners feared that their communities would be ruined if slavery were restricted or outlawed. As a result, many Southerners became suspicious of the federal (national) government, which they saw as a tool of the North. Southern leaders claimed that individual states should not have to take orders from the federal government about slavery or anything else.

This long-running feud finally broke open in 1861, after a Northerner named Abraham Lincoln (1809–1865) was elected president. Eleven Southern slaveholding states declared that they were leaving the United States and forming their own nation, called the Confederate States of America, or the Confederacy. But the states that remained loyal to the United States refused to accept this turn of events. These "Union" states vowed to keep the United States together as one nation. Before long, the two sides had gathered together great armies to settle their differences on the battlefield.

When the Civil War broke out, many free black men from the North tried to join the Union army. But the army turned them away, telling them that it was a "white man's war." "The answer from the War Department was always the same: no," wrote Mettger in *Till Victory Is Won.* "The Union army did not want the help of black men. The North was in the war to save the Union, not to end slavery."

During the war's early years, even President Lincoln opposed using black men as Union soldiers. Lincoln was morally opposed to slavery, but his main objective in going to war was to force the Southern states to rejoin the United States. He believed that using black soldiers might convince strategically important "border states" that the North was actually fighting to end slavery, not to restore the Union. "[Lincoln] wanted to retain the loyalty of the four slave states that had stayed in the Union when the war began—Kentucky, Maryland, Missouri, and Delaware," explained Mettger. "These states formed a valuable geographic buffer between the North and the Confederacy. If Lincoln broadened the scope of the war to include ending slavery in the rebel states, the border states might worry that he planned to outlaw slavery in their states as well and shift their allegiance to the Confederacy."

At first, the only war-related work that black men could find in the Union's army camps and navy piers was as common laborers. During the war's first months, most of these workers were free black men. But as the war dragged on, they were joined by large numbers of fugitive slaves from the South. This additional manpower greatly helped the North, but "even as the army came to depend on fugitive slave labor, the Union still was not ready to accept black men as soldiers," stated

Two escaped slaves sit in a Union army camp during the Civil War. *Courtesy of the Library of Congress.*

Black Sailors of the Civil War

Unlike the Union army, which showed great reluctance to accept black men within its ranks, the Union navy admitted black men only a few weeks after the war's first shots were fired. The war began in April 1861, when Confederate forces seized Fort Sumter, a federal military outpost located off the coast of South Carolina. By July 1861, Union navy recruiters were accepting free black men to fill sailor positions on battleships, gunboats, patrol boats, hospital ships, and other vessels. Some black personnel also worked in navy docks and shipyards. Some studies indicate that black men accounted for about eight percent of the total sailors in the Union navy.

Some ships were manned almost entirely by black crews.

Black sailors in the North also received better treatment than black soldiers in the army. For example, black sailors received the same pay as white sailors throughout the war. They also slept in the same sleeping area, ate at the same tables, and were given many of the same responsibilities as white navy personnel. This meant that black and white sailors alike worked on cannon crews, cleaned the ship, and took night guard duty.

According to historians, black sailors enjoyed greater equality and oppor-

Mettger. "The majority of white Northerners, although uncomfortable with the idea of one person owning another, did not believe in racial equality. Many were just as prejudiced as the average Southerner. African Americans were not allowed to vote in most free states and were banned from white churches and public facilities. Black children were barred from attending school with white children. Many Northerners simply did not believe that black men were smart enough, skilled enough, or brave enough to make good soldiers."

But America's black leadership refused to give up. Black leaders like Frederick Douglass (1817–1895) tirelessly lobbied President Lincoln and other political and military leaders, asking that black men be given an opportunity to serve their country as soldiers. They knew that if black men fought on behalf of the nation, America's political leaders would have to take notice. "Once let the black man get upon his person the

tunities in the navy for the simple reason that the limited size of ships forced black and white men to cooperate with one another, whether they were on or off duty. "The relative lack of discrimination resulted mainly from practical necessity," stated Zak Mettger in *Till Victory Is Won*. "There simply was not enough room on the ships to house and feed the men separately. The navy was also chronically short of men and could not afford to lose black sailors because of unfair treatment." Still, black sailors suffered from some forms of discrimination, even though they were risking their lives for the Union cause. They were not allowed to hold any rank higher than that of a sergeant. Some black crewmen worked under the threat of violence from racist white sailors.

Despite these negative factors, however, more than nineteen thousand free black men and escaped slaves served in the Union navy. By the time the war ended, about eight hundred of these sailors had been killed in action, and another two thousand had perished from disease. But just like in the army, blacks who served in the navy proved that they could be just as brave and skilled in battle as their white counterparts. In fact, eight black sailors who fought for the North received the U.S. Medal of Honor for extreme bravery in recognition of their conduct during the Civil War.

brass letter, U.S., let him get an eagle on his button, and a musket on his shoulder and bullets in his pocket, there is no power on earth that can deny that he has earned the right to citizenship," argued Douglass.

As the war dragged on with no end in sight, the idea of opening the army to black soldiers began to be taken more seriously. On July 17, 1862, Congress passed the Second Confiscation and Militia Act, freeing slaves whose masters were fighting in the Confederate army. A few months later, President Lincoln issued the Emancipation Proclamation, freeing all slaves in the Confederate states. After this declaration was issued, the Union army actively recruited black men for the war. It organized black men into all-black military units under the command of white officers. These regiments were filled with free black men from all across America, as well as thousands of runaway slaves.

Even after gaining admittance into the army, though, racial prejudice still dogged black soldiers. They received poor assignments, endured mistreatment by white officers and hostility from white troops, and were passed over for promotions that they deserved. "Black soldiers were reminded daily that the government they were fighting for valued them less than white soldiers," stated Mettger. "They were routinely given spoiled food, defective guns and poorly made uniforms. White troops, too, occasionally received substandard equipment and rations, but not as a general practice. . . . Black soldiers bitterly resented the unfair treatment."

This unfair treatment even extended to the pay that black soldiers received. In 1863, the standard monthly salary for a white enlisted man in the Union army was thirteen dollars a month, plus a three-dollar clothing allowance, for a sixteen-dollar monthly total. But black soldiers received only ten dollars a month, even though they put their lives at risk, too. In addition, the government deducted three dollars from their salaries for clothing, leaving them with a total of only seven dollars a month. This arrangement outraged both black soldiers and the growing number of white officers who recognized that they deserved equal pay. In fact, several black regiments protested the system by refusing to accept *any* pay until their salaries were made equal with those of white soldiers.

In August 1864, the U.S. Congress finally passed a law equalizing the pay of black soldiers and white soldiers. But this law applied only to black men who had been free when the war began. This meant that former slaves who joined the military were still being shortchanged, even though they were risking their lives for the Union cause. Finally, in March 1865—only one month before the war ended—a second law was passed granting equal pay to former slaves in the Union army.

By the time the war concluded, nearly 180,000 black men—about 10 percent of the Union's total troops—served in the Civil War. Of this total, nearly forty thousand black soldiers lost their lives in the conflict. The North's forces not only included all-black infantry regiments but also cavalry and artillery units composed entirely of black troops. Black soldiers also served in every major geographic region in which the war was fought, from the East Coast to the Deep South. Most importantly, black soldiers displayed their courage and mili-

tary skill on several notable occasions, including the 1863 assault on Fort Wagner, South Carolina, and the 1864 siege of Petersburg, Virginia. Their sacrifices on the battlefield helped "transform what began as a war to restore the Union into a struggle to end slavery," said Mettger.

"Black soldiers . . . perceived a great personal stake in the war," wrote James M. McPherson in *For Cause and Comrades: Why Men Fought in the Civil War.* "They fought for their own freedom, and beyond that for the freedom of all four million slaves. Many, especially those who had been free before the war, also fought for equal citizenship in a restored Union. Free and slave alike, they fought to prove their manhood in a society that prized courage as the hallmark of manhood. . . . By the war's last year, the example of black soldiers fighting for the Union as well as for liberty had helped convince most white soldiers that they should fight for black liberty as well as the Union."

Members of the Union army's 107th Colored Infantry, at Fort Corcoran, Washington, D.C.
Reproduced by permission of AP/Wide World Photos.

Black and white Union soldiers gather outside a tent during the Civil War.
Reproduced by permission of the Corbis Corporation.

Indeed, the attitudes of many prejudiced white Union soldiers changed as the war progressed. They recognized that the black soldiers were committed to achieving victory and that their inclusion in the army made it a much stronger force. By 1864, most white soldiers had dropped their opposition to black soldiers in the army. That year, President Lincoln ran for reelection on a pledge to abolish slavery everywhere in the United States. He received almost eighty percent of the vote from white Union soldiers.

Subject matter of *Till Victory Is Won*

Till Victory Is Won: Black Soldiers in the Civil War provides an overview of the black soldier's experience in the conflict. Mettger begins by explaining how black men were prohibited from serving in the Union army for the war's first two years, even though thousands of free blacks and escaped slaves desperately wanted to enlist. The book then discusses the Union's grudging decision to permit black soldiers.

Black men felt immense pride when they finally put on the uniform of the Union army. Military service gave them a chance to fight not only for their own freedom but for the freedom of black people all across the country. But even when the Union army decided to open its doors to black men, many racist attitudes and discriminatory rules remained in place. As the book continues, Mettger relates how black soldiers handled these challenges. For example, black recruits were usually given the most boring and tiresome duties. These orders spared them from bloodshed but also gave them no opportunity to strike a blow against slavery on the field of battle. As a result, many black soldiers waged a determined campaign to be treated as real soldiers, not just as camp workers. Another major problem for black Union soldiers was racism within the ranks. For example, many black troops received cruel treatment from racist white officers and soldiers. Finally, the author discusses the black soldiers' long and painful—but ultimately successful—struggle to receive the same monthly salary that was given to white soldiers.

Till Victory Is Won moves on to cover the most significant Civil War battles in which black soldiers participated. For example, Mettger tells readers about the soldiers of the Fifty-fourth Massachusetts. In April 1863, this all-black regiment led a heroic but doomed attack on a Confederate stronghold called Fort Wagner, in South Carolina. The fort's defenders successfully pushed back the assault, but the bravery shown by the men of the Fifty-fourth Massachusetts during the battle helped destroy the myth that black soldiers could not be good fighters.

The book's final chapters describe how black soldiers worked to provide for their families both during the war—when finding food and shelter was a daily struggle—and after

Cover of *Till Victory Is Won*. *Cover photo by Leib Image Archives, York, Pennsylvania. Front cover illustration, "Richmond, Virginia, April 2, 1865," reproduced by permission of Penguin Books, Ltd.*

Massacre at Fort Pillow

Tens of thousands of black men fought for the Union cause during the Civil War, even though the Confederate government promised to hand out especially harsh punishment to captured black soldiers. In fact, the Confederacy threatened to execute or enslave black Union soldiers caught during the war. In several cases, Southern forces followed through on these threats. The most famous of these incidents was the so-called "Fort Pillow Massacre."

Fort Pillow was located in Tennessee, on the east bank of the Mississippi River about forty miles north of Memphis. The fort had originally been built by Confederate forces in early 1862. But when the Confederate army abandoned it after a few weeks, Union forces occupied it with a small garrison of soldiers. The fort remained under Union control until April 1864. At that time, five hundred additional Union soldiers—most of them black—were sent to Fort Pillow to help defend it from an approaching Rebel force under the command of Nathan Bedford Forrest (1821–1877).

The reinforcements, however, could not prevent the Confederate army from seizing control of the fort. Forrest's forces attacked Fort Pillow on April 12. Before the day was over, Confederate troops had seized control of the fort and captured hundreds of Union soldiers. At that time, Forrest's men allegedly murdered hundreds of unarmed black Union soldiers in cold blood, as well as some white officers and soldiers. Reports of this terrible violence, which spared only 160 white and 40 black Union troops, quickly reached Northern communities. The North was outraged by the incident, and after the war the U.S. War Department launched an investigation into the massacre reports. The official investigation concluded that "the Confederates were guilty of atrocities [extremely evil or cruel acts] which included murdering most of the garrison after it surrendered, burying Negro soldiers alive, and setting fire to tents containing Federal [Union] wounded." More than a century later, the Fort Pillow Massacre continues to be regarded as one of the most terrible events of the war.

the war. This postwar period, known as Reconstruction in the South, was very difficult for black families, even though slavery had been eliminated from the United States. Many American laws still discriminated against black people, and racist attitudes remained strong in white communities, especially in the South. "Black veterans did not return to a perfect world," said Mettger. "Their shining performance in the army might have won them the respect of many whites, but it did not end

racism or poverty, both of which continued to oppress black Americans."

But according to Mettger, the Civil War experiences of black soldiers helped them meet those challenges. "Serving in the Union army . . . transformed the lives of black soldiers," Mettger wrote. "They had learned how to fight, not just against an armed enemy on the battlefield but also against less visible enemies such as injustice and racial discrimination. Soldiers took that knowledge home to their families and communities. . . . Thanks to their military experience, thousands of black men understood for the first time what it meant to be a citizen of the United States. They understood the rights and responsibilities that went with citizenship. They also had the will to push for those rights—for themselves, their families, and their communities. It was a struggle that thousands of black veterans would remain committed to for the rest of their lives."

This nineteenth-century illustration depicts the Fort Pillow Massacre in Tennessee. *Reproduced by permission of Archive Photos.*

"Spirit of Freedom" Honors Black Soldiers and Sailors

In July 1998, the United States unveiled the country's first monument dedicated exclusively to the black soldiers and sailors who fought for the Union cause during the Civil War. The eleven-foot-tall statue—called the "Spirit of Freedom"—shows several black Americans preparing for battle on land and at sea. "The African American soldiers who served in the Union army fought not only for the preservation of the Union but for their own freedom from slavery," said the ceremony's keynote speaker, Army lieutenant general Joe Ballard. "Perhaps more than any other men, these soldiers knew the value of freedom."

The monument is located in Washington, D.C., in the city's Shaw neighborhood. This predominantly black area is named after Colonel Robert Gould Shaw (1837–1863), the white officer who commanded the all-black Fifty-fourth Massachusetts regiment during the war. The memorial features plaques with the names of nearly 209,000 black Civil War soldiers and sailors and their white commanders.

"Spirit of Freedom" memorial in Washington, D.C. *Reproduced by permission of Leitha Etheridge-Sims.*

Two blocks from the "Spirit of Freedom" is the African American Civil War Memorial Museum, which provides information on the black soldiers' experience in the Civil War. Other displays in the museum cover America's slaveholding history and the abolitionist movement that helped put an end to the practice.

Style and themes in *Till Victory Is Won*

Author Zak Mettger arranged *Till Victory Is Won: Black Soldiers in the Civil War* in a simple, straightforward style. The book covers black soldiers' participation in the Civil War from the war's early days to its conclusion. As the work traces the history of black soldiers in the conflict, the author uses excerpts from letters and speeches written by black Americans to show how they felt about their involvement and their experiences.

The major purpose of Mettger's book is to show the amazing dedication and spirit of black Union soldiers during the Civil War. The Union army's black regiments were subjected to unfair treatment by their own government time and again, yet they continued to serve their country faithfully. They also received abusive treatment from white officers and fellow soldiers, even though they shared the burden of fighting the Confederate army. Yet despite these injustices and the ever-present threat of death on the battlefield, the Union's black soldiers performed well. In some cases, black regiments performed with true heroism, sacrificing their lives for the cause of freedom.

Research and Activity Ideas

1) Pretend that you are a free black man during the first months of the Civil War. Write a letter to President Lincoln urging him to allow black men into the Union army.

2) Even after fighting for the Union in the Civil War, black Americans were denied basic rights and treated unfairly by the nation's white-dominated society. For instance, black veterans were not even allowed to march in the Union's victory parade in Washington, D.C., when the war was over. Imagine that you are a black veteran who has just heard that the parade will exclude black regiments from participating. Compose a letter, a speech, or a journal entry that describes your feelings.

Related Titles

Dunbar, Paul Laurence. "The Colored Soldiers." *A poem honoring the black men who served in the Union Army during the Civil War.*

Glory. Tri-Star Pictures, 1989. *An Academy Award–nominated film that tells the story of the all-black 54th Massachusetts regiment and their white commander, Robert Gould Shaw.*

Hansen, Joyce. *Which Way Freedom.* New York: Walker, 1986. *In this novel, an African American boy escapes from slavery and joins a black regiment of the Union Army.*

Haskins, Jim. *Black, Blue, and Gray: African Americans in the Civil War.* New York: Simon & Schuster Books for Young Readers, 1998. *A nonfiction book that describes the contributions made by blacks on both sides of the conflict.*

Where to Learn More About . . .

Black Soldiers in the Civil War

Glatthaar, Joseph T. *Forged in Battle: The Civil War Alliance of Black Soldiers and White Soldiers*. New York: Meridian, 1991.

McPherson, James M. *For Cause and Comrades: Why Men Fought in the Civil War*. New York: Oxford University Press, 1997.

McPherson, James M. *The Negro's Civil War: How American Blacks Felt and Acted During the War for the Union*. New York: Ballantine, 1991.

McRae, Bennie J. Jr. *United States Colored Troops in the Civil War*. [Online] http://www.coax.net/people/lwf/data.htm (accessed on August 30, 2001).

Musicant, Ivan. *Divided Waters: The Naval History of the Civil War*. New York: HarperCollins, 1995.

Trudeau, Noah Andre. *Like Men of War: Black Troops in the Civil War, 1862–1865*. Boston: Little, Brown, 1998.

Where to Learn More

The following list of resources focuses on material appropriate for middle school or high school students. Please note that the Web site addresses were verified prior to publication, but are subject to change.

Books

Bradford, Ned, ed. *Battles and Leaders of the Civil War.* New York: New American Library, 1984.

Capaldi, Gina, and Alan Rockman. *Civil War: Garments, History, Legends, and Lore.* Torrance, CA: Good Apple, 1999.

Carter, Alden R. *The Civil War: American Tragedy.* New York: Franklin Watts, 1992.

Catton, Bruce. *The Civil War.* Boston: Houghton Mifflin, 1960.

Chang, Ina. *A Separate Battle: Women and the American Civil War.* New York: Scholastic, 1994.

Corrick, James A. *Life among the Soldiers and Cavalry.* San Diego: Lucent Books, 1999.

Hakim, Joy. *War, Terrible War.* 2nd ed. New York: Oxford University Press Children's Books, 1999.

Handlin, Oscar, and Lilian Handlin. *Abraham Lincoln and the Union.* Boston: Little Brown, 1980.

Hansen, Joyce. *Between Two Fires: Black Soldiers in the Civil War.* New York: Franklin Watts, 1993.

Haskins, J. *The Day Fort Sumter Was Fired On: A Photo History of the Civil War.* New York: Scholastic, 1994.

Lester, Julius. *To Be a Slave.* New York: Dial Press, 1968; rev. ed., 1998.

Murphy, Jim. *The Long Road to Gettysburg.* New York: Scholastic, 1995.

Seidman, Rachel Filene. *The Civil War: A History in Documents.* New York: Oxford University Press, 2000.

Sifakis, Stewart. *Who Was Who in the Civil War.* New York: Facts on File, 1988.

Stein, R. Conrad. *The Story of the Underground Railroad.* Chicago: Children's Press, 1981.

Ward, Geoffrey C., and Ken Burns. *The Civil War: An Illustrated History.* New York: Alfred A. Knopf, 1990.

Yancey, Diane. *Strategic Battles: The Civil War.* San Diego: Lucent Books, 1999.

Web Sites

AmericanCivilWar.com [Online] http://americancivilwar.com (accessed on September 24, 2001).

The Civil War for Kids. [Online] http://www2.lhric.org/pocantico/civilwar/cwar.htm (accessed on September 24, 2001).

Civil War in Miniature. [Online] http://civilwarmini.com/list.htm (accessed on September 24, 2001).

Hoemann, George H. *The American Civil War Homepage.* [Online] http://sunsite.utk.edu/civil-war (accessed on September 24, 2001).

Library of Congress. *Time Line of the Civil War.* [Online] http://memory.loc.gov/ammem/cwphtml/tl1861.html (accessed on September 24, 2001).

National Park Service, Civil War Soldiers & Sailors System. *African American History and the Civil War.* [Online] http://www.itd.nps.gov/cwss/history/aa_history.htm (accessed on September 24, 2001).

Rutgers University Libraries. *Civil War Resources on the Internet: Abolitionism to Reconstruction.* [Online] http://www.libraries.rutgers.edu/rul/rr_gateway/research_guides/history/civwar.shtml (accessed on September 24, 2001).

Watson, Kathie. *Poetry and Music of the War Between the States.* [Online] http://users.erols.com/kfraser (accessed on September 24, 2001).

Index

Note: *Italic* type indicates volume number; **boldface** indicates main entries and their page numbers; (ill.) indicates photos and illustrations.